Richard Garnett, Percy B. Shelley

Select letters.

Edited with an introd. by Richard Garnett

Richard Garnett, Percy B. Shelley

Select letters.

Edited with an introd. by Richard Garnett

ISBN/EAN: 9783337732400

Printed in Europe, USA, Canada, Australia, Japan

Cover: Foto ©ninafisch / pixelio.de

More available books at **www.hansebooks.com**

SELECT LETTERS

OF

PERCY BYSSHE SHELLEY

EDITED WITH AN INTRODUCTION BY

RICHARD GARNETT

NEW YORK
D. APPLETON AND COMPANY
1, 3, AND 5 BOND STREET
MDCCCLXXXII

INTRODUCTION

The publication of a book in the series of which this little volume forms part, implies a claim on its behalf to a perfection of form, as well as an attractiveness of subject, entitling it to the rank of a recognised English classic. This pretension can rarely be advanced in favour of familiar letters, written in haste for the information or entertainment of private friends. Such letters are frequently among the most delightful of literary compositions, but the stamp of absolute literary perfection is rarely impressed upon them.

The exceptions to this rule, in English literature at least, occur principally in the epistolary literature of the eighteenth century. Pope and Gray, artificial in their poetry, were not less artificial in their correspondence; but while in the former department of composition they strove to display their art, in the latter their no less successful endeavour was to conceal it. Together with Cowper and Walpole, they achieved the feat of imparting a literary value to ordinary topics by studious elaboration and precise nicety of expression, without at the same time sacrificing the familiar ease without which letters become rhetorical exercises. Such an achievement demanded more leisure and less absorbing emotion than fell to the lot of the succeeding age.

In the nineteenth century, accordingly, this artificial style of epistolary composition fell into disuse; letter-writing ceased to be an art among men of culture, and became more of the earnest practical thing which it had always been among men of business. It was now to be seen whether this gain in simplicity and sincerity was consistent with a high standard of epistolary polish. That age possessed many poets infinitely superior in genius to Cowper and Gray; but would their unpremeditated utterances, from a literary point of view, compare with the artifice of their predecessors? The answer is not doubtful. Byron, Scott, and Keats are excellent letter-writers, but their letters are far from possessing the classical impress which they communicated to their poetry. Much less is this the case with Wordsworth, Coleridge, Southey, or Landor. If that age had any master of epistolary composition among its wonderful poets, it was Shelley: Shelley or none.

Was Shelley such a master? The examples in this little volume will enable every one to judge for himself. Meanwhile the reader may be fairly asked to assume the fact as at least probable upon the testimony of an eminent modern critic, very refined indeed; fastidiously "jealous of dead leaves in the bay-wreath crown;" and, as will be seen, in most cases indisposed to dance to Shelley's piping. Mr. Matthew Arnold, in the preface to his "Selections from Byron's Poetry," "doubts whether Shelley's delightful Essays and Letters, which deserve to be far more read than they are now, will not resist the wear and tear of time better, and finally come to stand higher, than his poetry." This remarkable and, under present circumstances, highly seasonable deliverance will be weighed by those to whose lot it may fall to determine Mr. Arnold's own place as a critic; but need not be the subject of discussion here.

It will be sufficient to observe that, as a matter of fact, the general estimate of Shelley's prose will always conform nearly to the general estimate of his poetry. There is no such solution of continuity between the two as exists in the case of his illustrious contemporaries. Byron, for instance, writes verse like a poet, and prose like a man of the world. Shelley's letters are essentially and unmistakably the production of a poet, and compare with other celebrated letters precisely as his poems compare with other poetry. They do not, any more than his metrical compositions, represent every kind of excellence; but, like the latter, they have a high, rare, and peculiar excellence of their own. They have not the frankness of Byron's, the urbanity of Gray's, or the piquancy of Horace Walpole's. These merits, admirable as they are, are not characteristically poetical; the poet who displays them must for the time divest himself of his distinctive character as a poet; and of this Shelley was incapable. The peculiar virtue of his epistles is to express the mind of the poet as perfectly as Macaulay's express the mind of the man of letters, or Wellington's the mind of the general. Leaving disputable opinions out of account, and taking a comprehensive view of their general scope and spirit, they may be defined as a representation of the manner in which the poet, as such, contemplates life and nature; and a very great part of the pleasure to be derived from them is the observation of their intimate correspondence with the deliberate poetical achievement upon which they are an undesigned commentary.

They prove that Shelley's ideal world was a real world to Shelley himself; and contain nothing to suggest that the man habitually lived on a lower level than the author.

Most of the qualities of a good letter-writer were combined in Shelley, and Fortune also favoured the development of his genius in this direction. Such a writer must love his occupation for its own sake, irrespective of the quality of his correspondent. He must be genial and expansive, and not take the pen in hand with a misgiving that he may be wasting his time. It is even more important that he should be free from egotism, and capable, even while he writes about himself, of merging his own affairs in general interests and sympathies. Shelley complies with both these requisites in an unusual degree. It is further necessary that the writer should, as Mr. Arnold expresses it, have laid hold of the right subject-matter; and here again Shelley was fortunate. Fate had made him a sojourner in a land where the works of man vie with the works of nature; where the description of inanimate beauty may be relieved by constant reference to the productions of human genius, and nature and art alike are endeared to the cultivated observer or reader by a thousand associations and recollections.

A person gifted like Shelley could not write ill where Byron and De Staël had written well; but the truest charm of his letters is, after all, rather moral than literary. It is not so much the eloquence of the diction as the genuineness of the informing enthusiasm, the effusiveness of an opulent soul delighting in giving, and eager to impart the pleasure it has received. When not writing on Italy, Shelley is still most commonly fortunate in the subject of his letter, which derives interest either from something in the character or situation of the person to whom it is addressed, or from its reference to some adventure, or opinion, or production of his own. He is armed against triviality by never writing without a legitimate motive. He was by no means a regular or systematic correspondent, and before taking the pen in hand required the visitation of an emergency or an impulse. But such dictates of the spirit were frequent, and affected him like the impulses that prompt to poetical composition: nor was the product less distinctly an emanation of the intellect and the heart.

Such passages as the description of the Protestant cemetery (p. 81 of this collection), or the subtle interweaving of pleasurable feeling with even sweeter sadness in the last paragraph of the last letter Shelley wrote (p. 221), are lyrics in everything but structure. The former, indeed, has been expanded into a magnificent passage of the "Adonais;" and although to compare its sweet, brief note with the multitudinous harmonies of the elegy is, with Mr. Arnold's leave, like comparing the hymn of Pan to the hymn of Apollo, its music is not less truly poetry.

The main purpose of a selection adapted to the principle of a miniature library of masterpieces must be to reproduce whatever is most choice in the general body of Shelley's correspondence; an object involving the reproduction of nearly all the descriptions of Italian scenery and works of art addressed to Peacock, and those later letters, principally to Gisborne, which, if only by fitful glimpses, reveal a subtlety of mental introspection more exceptional than any brilliancy of word-painting. The former exhibit his powers of sustained eloquence in prose composition at their highest; the latter represent the development of his prose style, corresponding with that of his later lyrics, in the direction of intensity and transparency. The letters to Leigh Hunt and Horace Smith, less interesting psychologically, are still too important to be omitted, and the same remark applies to the six early letters to Miss Hitchener, selected, by the kind permission of the possessor, Mr. H. J. Slack, from a much more extensive collection. It cannot be expected that these juvenile effusions should be worthy of the maturer Shelley; they fall, indeed, far short of the standard which should, as a rule, be maintained in a selection like the present. They serve, nevertheless, as an appropriate prologue, displaying Shelley from the first in the character which, although with more dignity and modesty than his inexperience at that time permitted, he consistently supported to the last; while their biographical value is very considerable. Shelley's account of his marriage indicates what germs of estrangement lurked from the first in that ill-starred union; his appreciation of Southey is honourable to both; and his exposition of his religious opinions shows that Mr. Hogg was not wrong in calling " Queen Mab " a Platonic poem, and makes it more unaccountable than ever how he should, even in the midst of his youthful ferment, have fancied himself an atheist. A very few passages from these letters have been printed in the late Mr. Mac-

Carthy's interesting volume on "Shelley's Early Life" (1872).

The remainder of the Hitchener set of letters chiefly relate to Shelley's expedition to Ireland, an adventure so episodical that reference to it may well be omitted from a selection aiming before all things at harmonious completeness. The seventh letter, addressed to Mr. Hogg, was first printed by Mr. Forman, and though intrinsically unimportant, is in point of style and feeling a valuable link between the Hitchener letters and the letters from Italy. The latter are chiefly selected from those first published in Mrs. Shelley's edition of Shelley's prose works (1840), now out of print, and only accessible in the handsome but costly edition of Mr. Forman. A few, however, have been added from the "Shelley Memorials" and the supplementary collection published by Mr. Peacock in *Fraser's Magazine*. Two are entirely new: the deeply interesting account of little Allegra in her convent (No. XXXIX.), and the letter to Horace Smith (No. XLVII.), recovered by Mr. Forman's diligence from the Antipodes, and now published for the first time by his permission.

The total number of letters printed in Mr. Forman's edition is a hundred and twenty-seven, and forty or fifty more might be added from the "Shelley Memorials" and Mr. Hogg's biography; those derived from the latter source, however, with two or three remarkable exceptions, would hardly be worth reprinting. The present selection contains fifty-three, or between a third and a fourth of the whole, and includes nearly all those of any especial length or elaboration. The numerous curtailments which will be remarked follow in some instances the original editions, but have generally been made with deliberate reference to the character of this series of publications as a repository of choice things, and choice things only. With Shelley, indeed, distinction is the rule, commonplace the exception ; it has, nevertheless—bearing in mind that the purpose of this publication is not biographical but literary—been found desirable to omit numerous passages of merely personal interest. The text has never been tampered with, or the freedom of Shelley's utterance restrained, even when he touches upon religious subjects. To leave this side of his mind in obscurity would be unfair both to him and his readers; nor is there anything in the expression of his sentiments that can reasonably cause offence.

Mrs. Shelley's dramatic and circumstantial account of Shelley's death and the attendant occurrences was first published complete by Mr. Forman in *Macmillan's Magazine* for June, 1880. Some extracts had been given by the present Editor in the *Fortnightly Review* for June, 1878. It will be seen that his obligations both to Mr. Forman and to Mr. Slack are very considerable, and he is no less indebted to the generous aid of Mr. W. M. Rossetti.

R. GARNETT.

April 14, 1882.

SHELLEY'S LETTERS

I

To Miss Hitchener.

Mr. Strickland's, Blake St., York.
[*Saturday, 26 October, 1811 ?*]

. . . .

I hesitate not a moment to write to you : rare though it be in this existence, communion with you can unite mental benefit with *pure* gratification. I will explain, however, the circumstances which caused my marriage: these must certainly have caused much conjecture in your mind. Some time ago, when my sister was at Mrs. Fenning's school, she contracted an intimacy with Harriet. At that period I attentively watched over my sister, designing if possible, to add her to the list of the good, the disinterested, the free. I desired therefore to investigate Harriet's character; for which purpose I called on her, requested to correspond with her, designing that *her* advancement should keep pace with, and possibly accelerate, that of my sister. Her ready and frank acceptance of my proposal pleased me; and, though with ideas the remotest to those which have led to this conclusion of our intimacy, I continued to correspond with her for some time. The frequency of her letters became greater during my stay in Wales. I answered them: they became interesting. They contained complaints of the irrational conduct of her relatives, and the misery of living where she could *love* no one. Suicide was with her a favourite theme, and her total uselessness was urged as its defence. This I admitted supposing she could prove her inutility, and that she was powerless. Her letters became more and more gloomy. At length one assumed a tone of such despair as induced me to quit Wales precipitately. I arrived in London. I was shocked at observing the alteration of her looks. Little did I divine its cause : she had become violently attached to me, and feared that I should not return her attachment. Prejudice made the confession painful. It was impossible to avoid being much affected; I promised to unite my fate to her's. I stayed in London several days, during which she recovered her spirits. I had promised at her bidding to come again to London. They endeavoured to compel her to return to a school where malice and pride embittered every hour: she wrote to me. I came to London, I proposed marriage, for the reasons which I have given you, and she complied. Blame me if thou wilt, dearest friend, for *still* thou art dearest to me: yet pity even this error, if thou blamest me. If Harriet be not, at sixteen, all that you are at a more advanced age, assist me to mould a really noble soul into all that can make its nobleness useful and lovely. Lovely it is now, or I am the weakest slave to error.

P. B. S.

II

To Miss Hitchener.

Chesnut Cottage, Keswick.
[*Thursday, 11 November, 1811.*]

. . . . . .

What is love or friendship? Is it something material—a ball, an apple, a plaything—which must be taken from one and given to another? Is it capable of no extension, no communication? Lord Kaimes defines love to be a particularization of the general passion. But this is the love of sensation, of sentiment—the absurdest of absurd varieties: it is the love of pleasure, not the love of happiness. The one is a love which is self-centred, self-devoted, self-interested: it desires its own interest; it is the parent of jealousy. Its object is the plaything which it desires to monopolize. Selfishness, monopoly, is its very soul; and to communicate to others part of this love were to destroy its essence, to annihilate this chain of straw. But love, the love which *we* worship —virtue, heaven, disinterestedness—in a word Friendship—which has as much to do with the senses as with yonder mountains; that which seeks the good of all,—the good of its object first, not because that object is a minister to its pleasures, not merely because it even contributes to its happiness, but because it is really worthy, because it has powers, sensibilities, is capable of abstracting self, and loving virtue for virtue's own loveliness—desiring the happiness of others, not from the obligation of fearing hell or desiring heaven, but for pure, simple, unsophisticated virtue.

P. B. S.

III

To Miss Hitchener.

Keswick, Cumberland.
[*Sunday, 24 November, 1811.*]

. . . . . .

You talk of a future state: " is not this imagination" you ask " a proof of it"? To me it appears so, to me everything proves it. But what we earnestly desire we are very much prejudiced in favour of. It seems to me that everything lives again. What is the soul? Look at yonder flower. The blast of the north sweeps it from the earth; it withers beneath the breath of the destroyer. Yet that flower hath a soul: for what is soul but that which makes an organized being to be what it is, without which it would not be so? On this hypothesis must not that (the soul) without which a flower cannot be a flower exist, when the earthly flower hath perished? Yet where does it exist — in what state of being? Have not flowers also some end which nature destines their being able to answer? Doubtless, it ill becomes us to deny this, because we cannot certainly discover it; since so many analogies seem to favour the probability of this hypothesis.

I will say, then, that all nature is animated; that microscopic vision, as it has discovered to us millions of animated beings whose pursuits and passions are as eagerly followed as our own, so might it, if extended, find that nature itself was but a mass of organized animation. Perhaps the animative intellect of all this is in a constant rotation of change: perhaps a future state is no other than a different mode of terrestrial existence to which we have fitted ourselves in *this* mode.

Is there any probability in this supposition? On this plan, *congenial* souls *must* meet; because, having fitted themselves for nearly the same mode of being, they cannot fail to be *near* each other. Free-will must give energy to this infinite mass of being, and thereby constitute virtue. If *our* change be in this mortal life, do not fear that we shall be among the grovelling souls of heroes, aristocrats, and commercialists. Adieu.

P. B. S.

IV

To Miss Hitchener.

Keswick [*Sunday, 15 December, 1811*].

My dearest Friend,

You will before now have my last letter. I have felt the distrustful recurrences of the post-office which *you* felt when no answer to all your letters came. I have regretted that visit to Greystoke, because this delay must have given you uneasiness.

I have since heard from Captain P[ilfold]. His letter contains the account of a meditated proposal, on the part of my father and grandfather, to make my income immediately larger than the former's, in case I will consent to entail the estate on my eldest son, and, in default of issue, on my brother. Silly dotards! do they think I can be thus bribed and ground into an act of such contemptible injustice and inutility? that I will forswear my principles in consideration of 2000*l.* a year? that the goodwill I could thus purchase, or the ill-will I could thus overbear, would recompense me for the loss of self-esteem, of conscious rectitude? And with what face can they make me a proposal so insultingly hateful? Dare one of them propose such a condition to my face—to the face of any virtuous man—and not sink into nothing at his disdain? That I should entail 120,000*l.* of command over labour, of power to remit this, to employ it for beneficent purposes, on one whom I know not—who might, instead of being the benefactor of mankind, be its bane, or use this, for the worst purposes, which the real delegates of my chance-given property might convert into a most useful instrument of benevolence! No! this *you* will not suspect me of.

P. B. S.

V

To MISS HITCHENER.

Keswick [*Thursday, 26 December, 1811*].

MY DEAREST FRIEND,

I have delayed writing for two days that my letters might not succeed each other so closely as one day. I have also been much engaged in talking with Southey. You may conjecture that a man must possess high and estimable qualities if, with the prejudices of such total difference from my sentiments, I can regard him great and worthy. In fact, Southey is an advocate of liberty and equality. He looks forward to a state when all shall be perfected, and matter become subjected to the omnipotence of mind. But he is now an advocate for existing establishments. He says he designs his three statues in Kehama to be contemplated with republican feelings, but not in this age. Southey hates the Irish: he speaks against Catholic Emancipation and Parliamentary Reform. In all these things we differ, and our differences were the subject of a long conversation. Southey calls himself a Christian: but he does not believe that the Evangelists were inspired, he rejects the Trinity, and thinks that Jesus Christ stood precisely in the same relation to God as himself. Yet he calls himself a Christian. Now, if ever there was a definition of a Deist, I think it could never be clearer than this confession of faith. But Southey, though far from being a man of great reasoning powers, is a great man. He has all that characterises the poet; great eloquence, though obstinacy in opinion, which arguments are the last things that can shake. He is a man of virtue. He will never belie what he thinks, his professions are in compatibility with his practice. More of him another time.

With Calvert, the man whom I mentioned to you in that pygmy letter, we have now become acquainted. He knows everything that relates to my family and to myself: my expulsion from Oxford, the opinions that caused it, are no secrets to him. We first met Southey at his house. He has been very kind to us. The rent of our cottage was two guineas and a half a week with linen provided; he has made the proprietor lower it to one guinea, and has lent us linen himself.

P. B. S.

VI

To Miss Hitchener.

Keswick [*Thursday, 2 January, 1812*].

. . . . . .

I have lately had some conversation with Southey which has elicited my true opinions of God. He says I ought not to call myself an atheist, since in reality I believe that the Universe is God. I tell him I believe that " God " is another signification for " the Universe." I then explain:—I think reason and analogy seem to countenance the opinion that life is infinite; that, as the soul which now animates this frame was once the vivifying principle of the infinitely lowest link in the chain of existence, so is it ultimately destined to attain to the highest; that everything is animation (as explained in my last letter), and in consequence, being infinite, we can never arrive at its termination. How, on this hypothesis, are we to arrive at a First Cause?—Southey admits and believes this. Can he be a Christian? Can God be three? Southey agrees in my idea of Deity— the mass of infinite intelligence. I, you, and he, are constituent parts of the immeasurable whole.

What is now to be thought of Jesus Christ's divinity?

. . . . . .

Southey is no believer in original sin; he thinks that which appears to be a taint of our nature is in effect the result of unnatural political institutions. There we agree. He thinks the prejudices of education, and sinister influences of political institutions adequate to account for all the specimens of vice which have fallen within his observation.

You talk of Montgomery. We all sympathize with him, and often think and converse of him. I am going to write to him to-day. His story is a terrible one, it is briefly this—His father and mother were Moravian missionaries. They left this country to convert the Indians: they were young, enthusiastic, and excellent. The Indians savagely murdered them. Montgomery was then quite a child; but the impression of the event never wore away. When he grew up he became a disbeliever of Christianity, having very much such principles as a virtuous enquirer for truth. In the mean time he loved an apparently amiable female; he was about to marry her. Having some affairs in the West Indies, he went to settle them before his marriage. On his return to

Sheffield, he actually met the marriage procession of this woman, who had in the mean time chosen another love. He became melancholy mad; the horrible events of his life preyed upon his mind. He was shocked at having forsaken a faith for which a father and mother whom he loved had suffered martyrdom. The contest between his reason and his faith was destroying. He is now a Methodist. Will not this tale account for the melancholy and religious cast of his poetry? This is what Southey told me, word for word.

P. B. S<small>HELLEY</small>.

Southey says I am not an Atheist, but a Pantheist.

VII

To THOMAS JEFFERSON HOGG.

Bishopsgate [Windsor Forest, September, 1815].
MY DEAR FRIEND,
Your letter has lain by me for the last week, reproaching me every day. I found it on my return from a water excursion on the Thames, the particulars of which will have been recounted in another letter. The exercise and dissipation of mind attached to such an expedition have produced so favourable an effect on my health, that my habitual dejection and irritability have almost deserted me, and I can devote six hours in the day to study without difficulty. I have been engaged lately in the commencement of several literary plans, which, if my present temper of mind endures, I shall probably complete in the winter. I have consequently deserted Cicero, or proceed but slowly with his philosophic dialogues. I have read the oration for the poet Archias, and am only disappointed with its brevity.

I have been induced by one of the subjects which I am now pursuing to consult Bayle. I think he betrays an obliquity of understanding and coarseness of feeling. I have also read the four first books of Lucan's "Pharsalia," a poem as it appears to me of wonderful genius and transcending Virgil. Mary has finished the 5th book of the Aeneid, and her progress in Latin is such as to satisfy my best expectations.

The east wind—the wind of autumn—is abroad, and even now the leaves of the forest are shattered at every gust. When may we expect you? September is almost passed and October the month of your promised return is at hand, when we shall be happy to welcome you again to our fireside.

No events, as you know, disturb our tranquillity. Adieu.

Ever affectionately yours,
Percy B. Shelley.

VIII

To THOMAS LOVE PEACOCK.

Geneva, 17 July, 1816.

My opinion of turning to one spot of earth and calling it our home, and of the excellencies and usefulness of the sentiments arising out of this attachment, has at length produced in me the resolution of acquiring this possession.

You are the only man who has sufficient regard for me to take an interest in the fulfilment of this design, and whose tastes conform sufficiently to mine to engage me to confide the execution of it to your discretion.

I do not trouble you with apologies for giving you this commission. I require only rural exertions, walks, and circuitous wanderings, some slight negotiations about the letting of a house, the superintendence of a disorderly garden, some palings to be mended, some books to be removed and set up.

I wish you would get all my books and all my furniture from Bishopsgate, and all other effects appertaining to me. I have written to —— to secure all that belongs to me there to you. I have written also to Longdill to give up possession of the house on the 3rd of August.

When you have possessed yourself of all my affairs, I wish you to look out for a home for me and Mary and William, and the kitten who is now *en pension*. I wish you to get an unfurnished house, with as good a garden as may be, near Windsor Forest, and take a lease of it for fourteen or twenty-one years. The house must not be too small. I wish the situation to resemble as nearly as possible that of Bishopsgate, and should think that Sunning Hill or Winkfield Plain, or the neighbourhood of Virginia Water, would afford some possibilities.

My present intention is to return to England, and to make that most excellent of nations my perpetual resting place. I think it is extremely probable that we shall return next spring, perhaps before, perhaps after, but certainly we shall return.

On the motives and on the consequences of this journey, I reserve much explanation for some future winter walk or summer expedition. This much alone is certain, that before we return we shall have seen, and felt and heard, a multiplicity of things which will haunt our talk and make us a little better worth knowing than we were before our departure.

If possible, we think of descending the Danube in a boat, of visiting Constantinople and Athens, then Rome and the Tuscan cities, and returning by the South of France, always following great rivers, the Danube, the Po, the Rhone, and the Garonne : rivers are not like roads, the work of the hands of man ; they imitate mind, which wanders at will over pathless deserts, and flows through Nature's loveliest recesses, which are inaccessible to anything besides. They have the viler advantage also of affording a cheaper mode of conveyance.

This Eastern scheme is one which has just seized on our imaginations. I fear that the detail of execution will destroy it, as all other wild and beautiful visions ; but at all events you will hear from us wherever we are, and to whatever adventures destiny enforces us.

Tell me in return all English news. What has become of my poem ? I hope it has already sheltered itself in the bosom of its mother, Oblivion, from whose embraces no one could have been so barbarous as to tear it except me. Tell me of the political state of England. Its literature, of which when I speak Coleridge is in my thoughts —yourself lastly,—your own employments, your historical labours.

I had written thus far when your letter to Mary, dated the 8th, arrived. What you say of Bishopsgate of course modifies that part of this letter which relates to it. I confess I did not learn the destined ruin without some pain, but it is well for me perhaps that a situation requiring so large an expense should be placed beyond our hopes.

You must shelter my roofless Penates; dedicate some new temple to them, and perform the functions of a priest in my absence. They are innocent deities, and their worship neither sanguinary nor absurd. Leave Mammon and Jehovah to those who delight in wickedness and slavery—their altars are stained with blood, or polluted with gold, the price of blood. But the shrines of the Penates are good wood fires, or window frames intertwined with creeping plants; their hymns are the purring of kittens, the hissing of kettles, the long talks over the past and dead, the laugh of children, the warm wind of summer filling the quiet house, and the pelting storm of winter struggling in vain for entrance. In talking of the Penates, will you not liken me to Julius Cæsar dedicating a temple to Liberty?

As I have said in the former part of my letter, I trust entirely to your discretion on the subject of a house. Certainly the Forest engages my preference, because of the sylvan nature of the place, and the beasts with which it is filled. But I am not insensible to the beauties of the Thames, and any extraordinary eligibility of situation you mention in your letter would overbalance our habitual affection for the neighbourhood of Bishopsgate. Its proximity to the spot you have chosen is an argument with us in favour of the Thames. Recollect, however, we are now choosing a fixed, settled eternal home, and as such its internal qualities will affect us more constantly than those which consist in the surrounding scenery, which, whatever it may be at first, will shortly be no more than the colours with which our own habits shall invest it.

I am glad that circumstances do not permit the choice to be my own. I shall abide by yours as others abide by the necessity of their birth.

P. B. S.

IX

To William Godwin.

Marlow, 11 December, 1817.

I have read and considered all that you say about my general powers, and the particular instance of the poem in which I have attempted to develope them. Nothing can be more satisfactory to me than the interest which your admonitions express. But I think you are mistaken in some points with regard to the peculiar nature of my powers, whatever be their amount. I listened with deference and self-suspicion to your censures of Laon and Cythna; but the productions of mine which you commend hold a very low place in my own esteem, and this reassured me in some degree at least. The poem was produced by a series of thoughts which filled my mind with unbounded and sustained enthusiasm. I felt the precariousness of my life, and I resolved in this book to leave some record of myself. Much of what the volume contains was written with the same feeling, as real, though not so prophetic, as the communications of a dying man. I never presumed, indeed, to consider it anything approaching to faultless; but, when I considered contemporary productions of the same apparent pretensions, I will own that I was filled with confidence. I felt that in many respects it was a genuine picture of my own mind; I felt that the sentiments were true, not assumed, and in this have I long believed, that my power consists in sympathy, and that part of imagination which relates to sentiment and contemplation. I am formed, if for anything not in common with the herd of mankind, to apprehend minute and remote distinctions of feeling, whether relative to external nature or the living beings which surround us, and to communicate the conceptions which result from considering either the moral or the material universe as a whole . . . Yet, after all, I cannot but be conscious, in much of what I write, of an absence of that tranquillity which is the attribute and accompaniment of power. This feeling alone would make your most kind and wise admonitions on the subject of the economy of intellectual force valuable to me : and if I live, or if I see any trust in coming years, doubt not but that I shall do something, whatever it may be, which a serious and earnest estimate of my powers will suggest to me, and which will be in every respect accommodated to their utmost limits.

X

To THOMAS LOVE PEACOCK.

Milan, 20 April, 1818.

MY DEAR PEACOCK,

I had no conception that the distance between us, measured by time in respect of letters, was so great. I have but just received yours dated the 2nd, and when you will receive mine written from this city, somewhat later than the same date, I cannot know. I am sorry to hear that you have been obliged to remain at Marlow; a certain degree of society being almost a necessity of life, particularly as we are not to see you this summer in Italy. But this, I suppose, must be as it is. I often revisit Marlow in thought. The curse of this life is that whatever is once known can never be unknown. You inhabit a spot, which before you inhabit it, is as indifferent to you as any other spot upon earth, and when, persuaded by some necessity, you think to leave it, you leave it not; it clings to you, and with memories of things, which in your experience of them, gave no such promise, revenges your desertion. Time flows on, places are changed; friends who were with us are no longer with us; yet what has been seems yet to be, but barren and stripped of life. See, I have sent you a study for Nightmare Abbey.

Since I last wrote to you we have been to Como, looking for a house. This lake exceeds anything I ever beheld in beauty, with the exception of the Arbutus Islands in Killarney. It is long and narrow, and has the appearance of a mighty river winding among the mountains and forests. We sailed from the town of Como to a tract of country called the Tremezina, and saw the various aspects presented by that part of the lake. The mountains between Como and that village, or rather cluster of villages, are covered on high with chestnut forests, the eating chestnuts on which the inhabitants of the country subsist in time of scarcity, which sometimes descend to the very verge of the lake, overhanging it with their hoary branches. But usually the immediate border of this shore is composed of laurel-trees, and bay, and myrtle, and wild fig-trees, and olives, which grow in the crevices of the rocks, and overhang the caverns, and shadow the deep glens, which are filled with the flashing light of the waterfalls. Other flowering shrubs, which I cannot name, grow there also. On high, the towers of village churches are seen white among the dark forests. Beyond, on the opposite shore, which faces the south, the mountains descend less precipitously to the lake, and although they are much higher, and some covered with perpetual snow, there intervenes between them and the lake a range of lower hills, which have glens and rifts opening to the other, such as I should fancy the abysses of Ida or Parnassus. Here are plantations of olive, and orange, and lemon trees, which are now so loaded with fruit that there is more fruit than leaves; and vineyards. This shore of the lake is one continued village, and the Milanese nobility have their villas here. The union of culture and the untameable profusion and loveliness of nature is here so close that the line where they are divided can hardly be discovered. But the finest scenery is that of the Villa Pliniana, so called from a fountain which ebbs and flows every three hours, described by the younger Pliny, which is in the courtyard. This house, which was once a magnificent palace, and is now half in ruins, we are endeavouring to procure. It is built upon terraces raised from the bottom of the lake, together with its garden, at the foot of a semicircular precipice, overshadowed by profound forests of chestnut. The scene from the colonnade is the most extraordinary, at once, and the most lovely that eye ever beheld. On one side is the mountain, and immediately over you are clusters of cypress-trees of an astonishing height, which seem to pierce the sky. Above you, from among the clouds, as it were, descends a waterfall of immense size, broken by the woody rocks into a thousand channels to the lake. On the other side is seen the blue extent of the lake and the mountains, speckled with sails and spires. The apartments of the Pliniana are immensely large, but ill furnished and antique. The terraces, which overlook the lake, and conduct under the shade of such immense laurel-trees as deserve the epithet of Pythian, are most delightful. We stayed at Como two days, and have now returned to Milan, waiting the issue of our negotiation about a house. Como is only six leagues from Milan, and its mountains are seen from the cathedral.

This cathedral is a most astonishing work of art. It is built of white marble, and cut into pinnacles of immense height, and the utmost delicacy of workmanship, and loaded with sculpture. The effect of it, piercing the solid blue with those groups of dazzling spires, relieved by the serene depth of this Italian heaven, or by moonlight when the stars seem gathered among those clustered shapes, is beyond anything I had imagined architecture capable of producing. The interior, though very sublime, is of a more earthly character, and with its stained glass and massy granite columns overloaded with antique figures, and the silver lamps that burn for ever under the canopy of black cloth beside the brazen altar and the marble fretwork of the dome, give it the aspect of some gorgeous sepulchre. There is one solitary spot among those aisles, behind the altar, where the light of day is dim and yellow under the storied window, which I have chosen to visit, and read Dante there.

I have devoted this summer, and indeed the next year, to the composition of a tragedy on the subject of Tasso's madness, which I find upon inspection is, if properly treated, admirably dramatic and poetical. But, you will say, I have no dramatic talent; very true, in a certain sense; but I have taken the resolution to see what kind of a tragedy a person without dramatic talent could write. It shall be better morality than Fazio, and better poetry than Bertram, at least. You tell me nothing of Rhododaphne, a book from which, I confess, I expected extraordinary success.

P. B. S.

XI

To Mr. and Mrs. Gisborne.

Leghorn, Bagni di Lucca.
10 July, 1818.

You cannot know, as some friends in England do, to whom my silence is still more inexcusable, that this silence is no proof of forgetfulness or neglect.

I have, in truth, nothing to say, but that I shall be happy to see you again, and renew our delightful walks, until the desire or the duty of seeing new things hurries us away. We have spent a month here in our accustomed solitude, with the exception of one night at the Casino; and the choice society of all ages, which I took care to pack up in a large trunk before we left England, have revisited us here. I am employed just now, having little better to do, in translating into my faint and inefficient periods, the divine eloquence of Plato's Symposium; only as an exercise, or, perhaps, to give Mary some idea of the manners and feelings of the Athenians—so different on many subjects from that of any other community that ever existed.

We have almost finished Ariosto—who is entertaining and graceful, and *sometimes* a poet. Forgive me, worshippers of a more equal and tolerant divinity in poetry, if Ariosto pleases me less than you. Where is the gentle seriousness, the delicate sensibility, the calm and sustained energy, without which true greatness cannot be? He is so cruel, too, in his descriptions; his most prized virtues are vices almost without disguise. He constantly vindicates and embellishes revenge in its grossest form; the most deadly superstition that ever infested the world. How different from the tender and solemn enthusiasm of Petrarch—or even the delicate moral sensibility of Tasso, though somewhat obscured by an assumed and artificial style!

We read a good deal here—and we read little in Livorno. We have ridden, Mary and I, once only, to a place called Prato Fiorito, on the top of the mountains; the road, winding through forests and over torrents, and on the verge of green ravines, affords scenery magnificently fine. I cannot describe it to you, but bid you, though vainly, come and see. I take great delight in watching the changes of the atmosphere here, and the growth of the thunder showers with which the noon is often overshadowed, and which break and fade away towards evening into flocks of delicate clouds. Our fire-flies are fading fast away; but there is the planet Jupiter, who rises majestically over the rift in the forest-covered mountains to the south, and the pale summer lightning which is spread out every night, at intervals, over the sky. . . .

With the sentiment of impatience until we see you again in the autumn,

I am yours most sincerely,

P. B. SHELLEY.

XII

To Thomas Love Peacock.

Bagni di Lucca, 25 July, 1818.

My dear Peacock,

I received on the same day your letters marked five and six, the one directed to Pisa, and the other to Livorno, and I can assure you they are most welcome visitors.

Our life here is as unvaried by any external events as if we were at Marlow, where a sail up the river or a journey to London makes an epoch. Since I last wrote to you, I have ridden over to Lucca, once with Claire, and once alone; and we have been over to the Casino, where I cannot say there is anything remarkable, the women being far removed from anything which the most liberal annotator could interpret into beauty or grace, and apparently possessing no intellectual excellencies to compensate the deficiency. I assure you it is well that it is so, for these dances, especially the waltz, are so exquisitely beautiful that it would be a little dangerous to the newly unfrozen senses and imaginations of us migrators from the neighbourhood of the Pole. As it is— except in the dark—there could be no peril. The

atmosphere here, unlike that of the rest of Italy, is
diversified with clouds, which grow in the middle
of the day, and sometimes bring thunder and
lightning, and hail about the size of a pigeon's
egg, and decrease towards the evening, leaving
only those finely woven webs of vapour which
we see in English skies, and flocks of fleecy and
slowly-moving clouds, which all vanish before
sunset ; and the nights are for ever serene, and we
see a star in the east at sunset—I think it is
Jupiter—almost as fine as Venus was last summer;
but it wants a certain silver and aerial radiance,
and soft yet piercing splendour, which belongs, I
suppose, to the latter planet by virtue of its at
once divine and female nature. I have forgotten
to ask the ladies if Jupiter produces on them the
same effect. I take great delight in watching the
changes of the atmosphere. In the evening Mary
and I often take a ride, for horses are cheap in
this country. In the middle of the day, I bathe
in a pool or fountain, formed in the middle of
the forests by a torrent. It is surrounded on all
sides by precipitous rocks, and the waterfall of the
stream which forms it falls into it on one side
with perpetual dashing. Close to it, on the top
of the rocks, are alders, and, above, the great
chestnut trees, whose long and pointed leaves

pierce the deep blue sky in strong relief. The water of this pool, which, to venture an unrhythmical paraphrase, is "sixteen feet long and ten feet wide," is as transparent as the air, so that the stones and sand at the bottom seem, as it were, trembling in the light of noonday. It is exceedingly cold also. My custom is to undress and sit on the rocks, reading Herodotus, until the perspiration has subsided, and then to leap from the edge of the rock into this fountain—a practice in the hot weather exceedingly refreshing. This torrent is composed, as it were, of a succession of pools and waterfalls, up which I sometimes amuse myself by climbing when I bathe, and receiving the spray over all my body, whilst I clamber up the moist crags with difficulty.

I have lately found myself totally incapable of original composition. I have employed my mornings, therefore, in translating the Symposium, which I accomplished in ten days. Mary is now transcribing it, and I am writing a prefatory essay. I have been reading scarcely anything but Greek, and a little Italian poetry with Mary. We have finished Ariosto together—a thing I could not have done again alone.

"Frankenstein" seems to have been well re-

ceived, for although the unfriendly criticism of the
"Quarterly" is an evil for it, yet it proves that
it is read in some considerable degree, and it
would be difficult for them, with any appearance
of fairness, to deny it merit altogether. Their
notice of me, and their exposure of their true
motives for not noticing my book, show how
well understood an hostility must subsist between
me and them.

The news of the result of the elections, especially that of the metropolis, is highly inspiriting.
I received a letter, of two days later date, with
yours, which announced the unfortunate termination of that of Westmoreland. I wish you had
sent me some of the overflowing villany of those
apostates. What a pitiful wretch that Wordsworth: that such a man should be such a poet !
I can compare him with no one but Simonides,
that flatterer of the Sicilian tyrants, and at the
same time the most natural and tender of lyric
poets.

What pleasure would it have given me if the
wings of imagination could have divided the space
which divides us, and I could have been of your
party ! I have seen nothing so beautiful as Virginia
Water in its kind, and my thoughts for ever cling

to Windsor Forest, and the copses of Marlow, like the clouds which hang upon the woods of the mountains, low trailing, and though they pass away, leave their best dew when they themselves have faded.

XIII

To Thomas Love Peacock.

Bagni di Lucca, 16 August, 1818.

My dear Peacock,

No new event has been added to my life since I wrote last, at least none which might not have taken place as well on the banks of the Thames as on those of the Serchio. I project soon a short excursion, of a week or so, to some of the neighbouring cities, and on the 10th of September we leave this place for Florence, when I shall at least be able to tell you of some things which you cannot see from your windows.

I have finished, by taking advantage of a few days of inspiration—which the Camœnæ have been lately very backward in conceding—the little poem I began sending to the press in London. Ollier will send you the proofs. Its structure is slight and aery; its subject ideal. The metre corresponds with the spirit of the poem, and varies with the flow of the feeling. I have translated, and Mary has transcribed, the Symposium, as well as my poem, and I am proceeding to employ myself on a discourse upon the subject of which the Symposium treats, considering the subject with reference to the difference of sentiments respecting it existing between the Greeks and modern nations, a subject to be handled with that delicate caution which either I cannot or I will not practise in other matters, but which here I acknowledge to be necessary. Not that I have any serious thought of publishing either this discourse or the Symposium—at least till I return to England—when we may discuss the propriety of it.

"Nightmare Abbey" finished! Well, what is in it? What is it? You are as secret as if the priest of Ceres had dictated its sacred pages. However, I suppose I shall see in time, when my second parcel arrives. My first is yet absent. By what conveyance did you send it?

Pray, are you yet cured of your nympholepsy? 'Tis a sweet disease, but one as obstinate and dangerous as any, even when the nymph is a Poliad. Whether such should be the case or not, I hope your nympholeptic tale is not abandoned. The subject, if treated with a due spice of bacchic fury, and interwoven with the manners and feelings of those divine people, who, in their very errors, are the mirrors, as it were, in which all that is delicate and graceful contemplates itself, is perhaps equal to any. What a wonderful passage there is in Phædrus—the beginning, I think, of one of the speeches of Socrates—in praise of poetic madness, and in definition of what poetry is, and how a man becomes a poet! Every man who lives in this age and desires to write poetry, ought, as a preservative against the false and narrow systems of criticism which every poetical empiric vents, to impress himself with this sentence, if he would be numbered among those to whom may apply this proud, though sublime, expression of Tasso: "Non c'è in mondo chi merita nome di Creatore, che Dio ed il poeta."

The weather has been brilliantly fine, and now, among these mountains, the autumnal air is becoming less hot, especially in the mornings and evenings. The chestnut woods are now inexpressibly beautiful, for the chestnuts have become large, and add a new richness to the full foliage. We see here Jupiter in the east, and Venus, I believe, as the evening star, directly after sunset.

More and better in my next. Mary and Claire desire their kind remembrances.

Most faithfully your friend,
P. B. SHELLEY.

XIV

To Mrs. Shelley.

Bagni di Lucca, Florence.
Thursday, 11 o'clock [*20 August, 1818*].

DEAREST MARY,

We have been delayed in this city four hours for the Austrian minister's passport, but are now on the point of setting out with a vetturino, who engages to take us on the third day to Padua, that is, we shall only sleep three nights on the road. Yesterday's journey, performed in a one-horse cabriolet, almost without springs, over a rough road, was excessively fatiguing. Claire suffered most from it, for, as to myself, there are occasions in which fatigue seems a useful medicine, as I have felt no pain in my side—a most delightful respite—since I left you. The country was various and exceedingly beautiful. Sometimes there were those low cultivated lands, with their vine festoons, and large bunches of grapes just becoming purple, at others we passed between high mountains, crowned with some of the most majestic Gothic ruins I ever saw, which frowned from the bare precipices, or were half seen among the olive copses. As we approached Florence, the country became cultivated to a very high degree; the plain was filled with the most beautiful villas, and as far as the eye could reach the mountains were covered with them, for the plains are bounded on all sides by blue and misty mountains. The vines are here trailed on low trellises of reeds interwoven into crosses to support them, and the grapes, now almost ripe, are exceedingly abundant. You everywhere meet those teams of beautiful white oxen, which are now labouring the little vine-divided fields with their Virgilian ploughs and carts. Florence itself, that is the Lung' Arno, for I have seen no more, I think is the most beautiful city I have yet seen. It is surrounded with cultivated hills, and from the bridge which crosses the broad channel of the Arno the view is the most animated and elegant I ever saw. You see three or four bridges apparently supported by Corinthian pillars, and the white sails of the boats, relieved by the deep green of the forest, which comes to the water's edge, and the sloping hills covered with bright villas on every side. Domes and steeples rise on all sides, and the cleanliness is remarkably great. On the other side there are the foldings of the vale of Arno above, first the hills of olive and vine, then the chestnut woods, and then the blue and misty pine forests, which invest the aerial Apennines, that fade in the distance. I have seldom seen a city so lovely at first sight as Florence.

We shall travel hence within a few hours, with the speed of the post, since the distance is 190 miles, and we are to do it in three days, besides the half day, which is somewhat more than sixty miles a day. We have now got a comfortable carriage and two mules, and, thanks to Paolo, have made a very decent bargain, comprising everything, to Padua. I should say we had delightful fruit for breakfast—figs, very fine, and peaches, unfortunately gathered before they were ripe, whose smell was like what one fancies of the wakening of paradise flowers.

Well, my dearest Mary, are you very lonely? Tell me truth, my sweetest, do you ever cry? I shall hear from you once at Venice, and once on my return here. If you love me, you will keep up your spirits, and, at all events, tell me truth about it, for, I assure you, I am not of a disposition to be flattered by your sorrow, though I should be by your cheerfulness, and, above all, by seeing such fruits of my absence as were produced when we were at Geneva. What acquaintances have you made? I might have travelled to Padua with a German, who had just come from Rome, and had scarce recovered from a malaria fever, caught in the Pontine Marshes a week or two since; and I conceded to Claire's entreaties, and to your absent suggestions, and omitted the opportunity, although I have no great faith in such species of contagion. It is not very hot, not at all too much so for my sensations, and the only thing that incommodes me are the gnats at night, who roar like so many humming tops in one's ear, and I do not always find zanzariere. How is Willmouse and little Clara? They must be kissed for me, and you must particularly remember to speak my name to William, and see that he does not quite forget me before I return. Adieu, my dearest girl, I think that we shall soon meet. I shall write again from Venice. Adieu, dear Mary!

I have been reading the "Noble Kinsmen," in which, with the exception of that lovely scene to which you added so much grace in reading to me, I have been disappointed. The jailor's daughter is a poor imitation, and deformed. The whole story wants moral discrimination and modesty. I do not believe Shakespeare wrote a word of it.

XV

To MRS. SHELLEY.

Bagni di Lucca, Venice.
Sunday morning [*23 August, 1818*].

MY DEAREST MARY,

We arrived here last night at twelve o'clock, and it is now before breakfast the next morning. I can, of course, tell you nothing of the future, and though I shall not close this letter till post time, yet I do not know exactly when that is. Yet, if you are very impatient, look along the letter and you will see another date, when I may have something to relate. . . . .

We came from Padua hither in a gondola, and the gondoliere, among other things, without any hint on my part, began talking of Lord Byron. He said he was a *giovinetto Inglese*, with a *nome stravagante*, who lived very luxuriously, and spent great sums of money. This man, it seems, was one of Lord Byron's gondolieri. No sooner had we arrived at the inn than the waiter began talking about him—said that he frequented Mrs. Hoppner's conversazioni very much.

Our journey from Florence to Padua contained

nothing which may not be related another time. At Padua, as I said, we took a gondola, and left it at three o'clock. These gondolas are the most convenient and beautiful boats in the world. They are finely carpeted and furnished with black and painted black. The couches upon which you lean are extraordinarily soft, and are so disposed as to be the most comfortable to those who lean or sit. The windows have at will either Venetian plate-glass flowered, or Venetian blinds, or blinds of black cloth to shut out the light. The weather here is extremely cold ; indeed, sometimes very painfully so, and yesterday it began to rain. We passed the Laguna in the middle of the night in a most violent storm of wind, rain and lightning. It was very curious to observe the elements above in a state of such tremendous convulsions, and the surface of the water almost calm ; for these lagunas, though five miles broad—a space enough in a storm to sink any gondola—are so shallow that the boatmen drive the boat along with a pole. The sea-water, furiously agitated by the wind, shone with sparkles like stars. Venice, now hidden and now disclosed by the driving rain, shone dimly with its lights. We were all this while safe and comfortable, except that Claire was now and then a little frightened in our cabin. Well, adieu, dearest : I shall, as Miss Byron says, resume the pen in the evening. . . .

At three o'clock I called on Lord Byron; he was delighted to see me, and our first conversation of course consisted in the object of my visit. . . .

Well, my dear Mary, this talk went off, for I did not see in that moment how I could urge it further, and I thought that at least many points were gained in the willingness and good humour of our discussion. So he took me in his gondola —much against my will, for I wanted to return to Claire at the Hoppners'—across the Laguna to a long sandy island, which defends Venice from the Adriatic. When we disembarked, we found his horses waiting for us, and we rode along the sands of the sea talking. Our conversation consisted in the history of his wounded feelings, and questions as to my affairs, and great professions of friendship and regard for me. He said that if he had been in England at the time of the chancery affair, he would have moved heaven and earth to have prevented such a decision. We talked of literary matters—his fourth Canto, which he says is very good, and, indeed, repeated some stanzas of great energy to me—when we returned to his palace. . . .

Do you know, dearest, how this letter was written? By scraps and patches, and interrupted every minute. The gondola is now come to take us up to Fusina. Este is a little place, and the house found without difficulty. I shall count four days for this letter: one day for packing, four for coming here, and on the ninth or tenth day we shall meet.

I am too late for the post, but I send an express to overtake it. Enclosed is an order for 50*l*. If you knew all that I had to do!

Dearest love, be well, be happy; come to me, and confide in your own constant and affectionate
P. B. S.

Kiss the blue-eyed darlings for me, and don't let William forget me. Clara cannot recollect me.

XVI

To Thomas Love Peacock.

Este, [*8 October, 1818.*]

My dear Peacock,

I have not written to you, I think, for six weeks, but I have often felt that I had many things to say; but I have not been without events to disturb and distract me, amongst which is the death of my little girl. She died of a disorder peculiar to the climate. We have all had bad spirits enough, and I, in addition, bad health. I intend to be better soon; there is no malady, bodily or mental, which does not either kill or is killed.

We left the baths of Lucca, I think, the day after I wrote to you, on a visit to Venice, partly for the sake of seeing the city. We made a very delightful acquaintance there with a Mr. and Mrs. Hoppner, the gentleman an Englishman, and the lady a Swissesse, mild and beautiful, and unprejudiced, in the best sense of the word. The kind attentions of these people made our short stay at Venice very pleasant. I saw Lord Byron, and really hardly knew him again: he is changed into the liveliest and happiest-looking man I ever met. He read me the first canto of his "Don Juan," a thing in the style of "Beppo," but infinitely better, and dedicated to Southey in ten or a dozen stanzas, more like a mixture of wormwood and verdigris than satire. Venice is a wonderfully fine city. The approach to it over the Laguna, with its domes and turrets glittering in a long line over the blue waves, is one of the finest architectural delusions in the world. It seems to have, and literally it has, its foundations in the sea. The silent streets are paved with water, and you hear nothing but the dashing of the oars, and the occasional cries of the gondolieri. I heard nothing of Tasso. The gondolas themselves are things of a most romantic and picturesque appearance; I can only compare them to moths, of which a coffin might have been the chrysalis. They are hung with black, and painted black, and carpeted with grey; they curl at the prow and stern, and at the former there is a nondescript beak of shining steel, which glitters at the end of its long black mass.

The Doge's palace, with its library, is a fine monument of aristocratic power. I saw the dungeons, where these scoundrels used to torment their victims. They are of three kinds, one adjoining the place of trial, where the prisoners destined to immediate execution were kept. I could not descend to them, because the day on which I visited it was festa. Another under the leads of the palace, where the sufferers were roasted to death or madness by the ardours of an Italian sun; and others, called the Pozzi—or wells, deep underneath, and communicating with those on the roof by secret passages—where the prisoners were confined sometimes half up to their middles in stinking water. When the French came here they found only one old man in the dungeons, and he could not speak. But Venice, which was once a tyrant, is now the next worse thing, a slave; for, in fact, it ceased to be free, or worth our regret as a nation, from the moment that the oligarchy usurped the rights of the people; yet, I do not imagine that it was ever so degraded as it has been since the French, and especially the Austrian yoke. The Austrians take sixty per cent. in taxes, and impose free quarters on the inhabitants. A horde of German soldiers, as vicious and more disgusting than the Venetians themselves, insult these miserable people. I had no conception of the excess to which avarice, cowardice, superstition, ignorance, passionless lust, and all the inexpressible brutalities which degrade human nature, could be carried, until I had passed a few days at Venice.

We have been living this last month near the little town from which I date this letter, in a very pleasant villa which has been lent to us, and we are now on the point of proceeding to Florence, Rome, and Naples, at which last city we shall spend the winter, and return northwards in the spring. Behind us here are the Euganean Hills, not so beautiful as those of the Bagni di Lucca, with Arquà, where Petrarch's house and tomb are religiously preserved and visited. At the end of our garden is an extensive gothic castle, now the habitation of owls and bats, where the Medici family resided before they came to Florence. We see before us the wide flat plains of Lombardy, in which we see the sun and moon rise and set, and the evening star, and all the golden magnificence of autumnal clouds. But I reserve wonder for Naples.

I have been writing, and indeed have just finished the first act of, a lyric and classical drama, to be called " Prometheus Unbound." Will you tell me what there is in Cicero about a drama supposed to have been written by Aeschylus under this title ?

I ought to say that I have just read Malthus in a French translation. Malthus is a very clever man, and the world would be a great gainer if it would seriously take his lessons into consideration, if it were capable of attending seriously to anything but mischief—but what on earth does he mean by some of his inferences!

Yours ever faithfully,
P. B. S.

XVII

To THOMAS LOVE PEACOCK.

Ferrara, 8 November, 1818.

MY DEAR PEACOCK,

We left Este yesterday on our journey towards Naples. The roads were particularly bad; we have, therefore, accomplished only two days' journey, of eighteen and twenty-four miles each, and you may imagine that our horses must be tolerably good ones, to drag our carriage, with five people and heavy luggage, through deep and clayey roads. The roads are, however, good during the rest of the way.

The country is flat, but intersected by lines of wood, trellised with vines, whose broad leaves are now stamped with the redness of their decay. Every here and there one sees people employed in agricultural labours, and the plough, the harrow, or the cart, drawn by long teams of milk-white or dove-coloured oxen of immense size and exquisite beauty. This, indeed, might be the country of Pasiphaes. In one farmyard I was shown sixty-three of these lovely oxen, tied to their stalls, in excellent condition. A farmyard in this part of Italy is somewhat different from one in England.

First, the house, which is large and high, with strange-looking unpainted window-shutters, generally closed, and dreary beyond conception. The farmyard and out-buildings, however, are usually in the neatest order. The threshing-floor is not under cover, but like that described in the " Georgics," usually flattened by a broken column, and neither the mole, nor the toad, nor the ant, can find on its area a crevice for their dwelling. Around it, at this season, are piled the stacks of the leaves and stalks of Indian corn, which has lately been threshed and dried upon its surface. At a little distance are vast heaps of many-coloured zucche or pumpkins, some of enormous size, piled as winter food for the hogs. There are turkeys, too, and fowls wandering about, and two or three dogs, who bark with a sharp hylactism. The people who are occupied with the care of these things seem neither ill-clothed nor ill-fed, and the blunt incivility of their manners has an English air with it, very discouraging to those who are accustomed to the impudent and polished lying of the inhabitants of the cities. I should judge the agricultural resources of this country to be immense, since it can wear so flourishing an appearance, in spite of the enormous discouragements which the various tyranny of the governments inflicts on it. I ought to say that one of the farms belongs to a Jew banker at Venice—another Shylock. We arrived late at the inn where I now write; it was once the palace of a Venetian nobleman, and is now an excellent inn. To-morrow we are going to see the sights of Ferrara.

9 November.

We have had heavy rain and thunder all night, and the former still continuing, we went in the carriage about the town. We went first to look at the cathedral, but the beggars very soon made us sound a retreat; so, whether, as it is said, there is a copy of a picture of Michael Angelo there or no, I cannot tell. At the public library we were more successful. This is, indeed, a magnificent establishment, containing, as they say, 160,000 volumes. We saw some illuminated manuscripts of church music, with the verses of the Psalms interlined between the square notes, each of which consisted of the most delicate tracery, in colours inconceivably vivid. They belonged to the neighbouring convent of Certosa, and are three or four hundred years old, but their hues are as fresh as if they had been executed yesterday. The tomb of Ariosto occupies one end of the largest saloon of which the library is composed; it is formed of various marbles, surmounted by an expressive bust of the poet, and subscribed with a few Latin verses, in a less miserable taste than those usually employed for similar purposes. But the most interesting exhibitions here are the writings, &c., of Ariosto and Tasso, which are preserved, and were concealed from the undistinguishing depredations of the French with pious care. There is the arm-chair of Ariosto, an old plain wooden piece of furniture, the hard seat of which was once occupied by— but has now survived—its cushion, as it has its master. I could fancy Ariosto sitting in it, and the satires in his own handwriting, which they unfold beside it, and the old bronze inkstand, loaded with figures, which belonged also to him, assist the willing delusion. This inkstand has an antique, rather than an ancient appearance. Three nymphs lean forth from the circumference, and on the top of the lid stands a Cupid, winged and looking up, with a torch in one hand, his bow in the other, and his quiver beside him. A medal was bound round the skeleton of Ariosto, with his likeness impressed upon it. I cannot say I think it had much native expression, but perhaps the artist was in fault. On the reverse is a hand, cutting, with a pair of scissors, the tongue from a serpent, upraised from the grass, with this legend, *pro bono malum*. What this reverse of the boasted Christian maxim means, or how it applies to Ariosto, either as a satirist or a serious writer, I cannot exactly tell. The cicerone attempted to explain, and it is to his commentary that my bewildering is probably due—if, indeed, the meaning be very plain, as is possibly the case.

There is here a manuscript of the entire "Gerusalemme Liberata," written by Tasso's own hand; a manuscript of some poems, written in prison, to the Duke Alfonso; and the satires of Ariosto, written also by his own hand; and the "Pastor Fido" of Guarini. The "Gerusalemme," though it had evidently been copied and recopied, is interlined, particularly towards the end, with numerous corrections. The handwriting of Ariosto is a small, firm, and pointed character, expressing, as I should say, a strong and keen but circumscribed energy of mind; that of Tasso is large, free, and flowing, except that there is a checked expression in the midst of its flow, which brings the letters into a smaller compass than one expected from the beginning of the word. It is the symbol of an intense and earnest mind, exceeding at times its own depth, and admonished to return by the chillness of the waters of oblivion striking upon its adventurous feet. You know I always seek in what I see the manifestation of something beyond the present and tangible object; and as we do not agree in physiognomy, so we may not agree now. But my business is to relate my own sensations, and not to attempt to inspire others with them. Some of the MSS. of Tasso were sonnets to his persecutor, which contain a great deal of what is called flattery. If Alfonso's ghost were asked how he felt those praises now, I wonder what he would say. But to me there is much more to pity than to condemn in these entreaties and praises of Tasso. It is as a bigot prays to and praises his God, whom he knows to be the most remorseless, capricious, and inflexible of tyrants, but whom he knows also to be omnipotent. Tasso's situation was widely different from that of any persecuted being of the present day, for from the depth of dungeons, public opinion might now at length be awakened to an echo that would startle the oppressor. But then there was no hope. There is something irresistibly pathetic to me in the sight of Tasso's own handwriting, moulding expressions of adulation and entreaty to a deaf and stupid tyrant, in an age when the most heroic virtue would have exposed its possessor to hopeless persecution, and —such is the alliance between virtue and genius— which unoffending genius could not escape.

We went afterwards to see his prison in the hospital of Sant' Anna, and I enclose you a piece of wood of the very door which for seven years and three months divided this glorious being from the air and the light which had nourished in him those influences which he has communicated, through his poetry, to thousands. The dungeon is low and dark, and, when I say that it is really a very decent dungeon, I speak as one who has seen the prisons in the Doge's palace at Venice. But it is a horrible abode for the coarsest and meanest thing that ever wore the shape of man, much more for one of delicate susceptibilities and elevated fancies. It is low, and has a grated window, and being sunk some feet below the level of the earth, is full of unwholesome damps. In the darkest corner is a mark in the wall, where the chains were rivetted which bound him hand and foot. After some time, at the instance of some cardinal his friend, the duke allowed his victim a fireplace; the mark where it was walled up yet remains.

At the entrance of the Liceo, where the library is, we were met by a penitent; his form was completely enveloped in ghost-like drapery of white flannel; his bare feet were sandalled, and there was a kind of network visor drawn over his eyes, so as entirely to conceal his face. I imagine that this man had been adjudged to suffer this penance for some crime known only to himself and his confessor, and this kind of exhibition is a striking instance of the power of the Catholic superstition over the human mind. He passed, rattling his wooden box for charity.

Adieu. You will hear from me again before I arrive at Naples.

Yours ever sincerely,
P. B. S.

XVIII

TO THOMAS LOVE PEACOCK.

Bologna, Monday, 9 November, 1818.

MY DEAR PEACOCK,

I have seen a quantity of things here—churches, palaces, statues, fountains, and pictures; and my brain is at this moment like a portfolio of an architect, or a print-shop, or a common-place book. I will try to recollect something of what I have seen; for indeed it requires, if it will obey, an act of volition. First we went to the cathedral, which contains nothing remarkable, except a kind of shrine, or rather a marble canopy, loaded with sculptures, and supported on four marble columns. We went then to a palace—I am sure I forget the name of it—where we saw a large gallery of pictures. Of course, in a picture-gallery you see three hundred pictures you forget for one you remember. I remember, however, an interesting picture by Guido of the "Rape of Proserpine," in which Proserpine casts back her languid and half-unwilling eyes, as it were, to the flowers she had left ungathered in the fields of Enna. There was an exquisitely executed piece of Correggio, about four saints, one of whom seemed to have a pet dragon in a leash. I was told that it was the devil who was bound in that style—but who can make anything of four saints? For what can they be supposed to be about? There was one painting, indeed, by this master, "Christ beatified," inexpressibly fine. It is a half figure, seated on a mass of clouds, tinged with an aetherial, rose-like lustre; the arms are expanded; the whole frame seems dilated with expression; the countenance is heavy, as it were, with the rapture of the spirit; the lips parted, but scarcely parted, with the breath of intense but regulated passion; the eyes are calm and benignant; the whole features harmonized in majesty and sweetness. The hair is parted on the forehead, and falls in heavy locks on each side. It is motionless, but seems as if the faintest breath would move it. The colouring, I suppose, must be very good, if I could remark and understand it. The sky is of a pale aerial orange, like the tints of latest sunset; it does not seem painted around and beyond the figure, but everything seems to have absorbed and to have been penetrated by its hues. I do not think we saw any other of Correggio, but this specimen gives me a very exalted idea of his powers.

We went to see heaven knows how many more palaces—Ranuzzi, Marriscalchi, Aldobrandi.

If you want Italian names for any purpose, here they are; I should be glad of them if I was writing a novel. I saw many more of Guido. One a Samson drinking water out of an ass's jawbone, in the midst of the slaughtered Philistines. Why he is supposed to do this, God, who gave him this jaw-bone, alone knows—but certain it is that the painting is a very fine one. The figure of Samson stands in strong relief in the foreground, coloured, as it were, in the hues of human life, and full of strength and elegance. Round him lie the Philistines in all the attitudes of death. One prone, with the slight convulsion of pain just passing from his forehead, whilst on his lips and chin death lies as heavy as sleep. Another leaning on his arm, with his hand, white and motionless, hanging out beyond. In the distance, more dead bodies; and, still further beyond, the blue sea and the blue mountains, and one white and tranquil sail.

There is a " Murder of the Innocents," also by Guido, finely coloured, with much fine expression—but the subject is very horrible, and it seemed deficient in strength—at least, you require the highest ideal energy, the most poetical and exalted conception of the subject, to reconcile you to such a contemplation. There was a " Jesus

Christ crucified" by the same, very fine. One gets tired, indeed, whatever may be the conception and execution of it, of seeing that monotonous and agonized form for ever exhibited in one prescriptive attitude of torture. But the Magdalen, clinging to the cross with the look of passive and gentle despair beaming from beneath her bright flaxen hair, and the figure of St. John, with his looks uplifted in passionate compassion; his hands clasped, and his fingers twisting themselves together, as it were, with involuntary anguish; his feet almost writhing up from the ground with the same sympathy; and the whole of this arrayed in colours of a diviner nature, yet most like nature's self—of the contemplation of this one would never weary.

There was a "Fortune," too, of Guido; a piece of mere beauty. There was the figure of Fortune on a globe, eagerly proceeding onwards, and Love was trying to catch her back by the hair, and her face was half turned towards him; her long chestnut hair was floating in the stream of the wind, and threw its shadow over her fair forehead. Her hazel eyes were fixed on her pursuer with a meaning look of playfulness, and a light smile was hovering on her lips. The colours which arrayed her delicate limbs were aetherial and warm.

But, perhaps, the most interesting of all the pictures of Guido which I saw was a " Madonna Lattante." She is leaning over her child, and the maternal feelings with which she is pervaded are shadowed forth on her soft and gentle countenance, and in her simple and affectionate gestures. There is what an unfeeling observer would call a dullness in the expression of her face; her eyes are almost closed; her lip depressed; there is a serious, and even a heavy relaxation, as it were, of all the muscles which are called into action by ordinary emotions; but it is only as if the spirit of love, almost insupportable from its intensity, were brooding over, and weighing down the soul, or whatever it is, without which the material frame is inanimate and inexpressive.

There is another painter here, called Franceschini, a Bolognese, who, though certainly very inferior to Guido, is yet a person of excellent powers. One entire church, that of Santa Catarina, is covered by his works. I do not know whether any of his pictures have ever been seen in England. His colouring is less warm than that of Guido, but nothing can be more clear and delicate; it is as if he could have dipped his pencil in the hues of some serenest and star-shining twilight. His forms have the same delicacy and aerial loveliness; their eyes are all bright with innocence and love; their lips scarce divided by some gentle and sweet emotion. His winged children are the loveliest ideal beings ever created by the human mind. These are generally, whether in the capacity of cherubim or Cupid, accessories to the rest of the picture; and the underplot of their lovely and infantine play is something almost pathetic, from the excess of its unpretending beauty. One of the best of his pieces is an Annunciation of the Virgin; the angel is beaming in beauty; the Virgin, soft, retiring, and simple.

We saw, besides, one picture of Raphael—St. Cecilia; this is in another and higher style; you forget that it is a picture as you look at it; and yet it is most unlike any of those things which we call reality. It is one of the inspired and ideal kind, and seems to have been conceived and executed in a similar state of feeling to that which produced among the ancients those perfect specimens of poetry and sculpture which are the baffling models of succeeding generations. There is an unity and a perfection in it of an incommunicable kind. The central figure, St. Cecilia, seems rapt in such inspiration as produced her image in the painter's mind; her deep, dark, eloquent eyes lifted up; her chestnut hair flung back from her forehead—she holds an organ in her hands—her countenance, as it were, calmed by the depth of its passion and rapture, and penetrated throughout with the warm and radiant light of life. She is listening to the music of heaven, and, as I imagine, has just ceased to sing, for the four figures that surround her evidently point, by their attitudes, towards her; particularly St. John, who, with a tender yet impassioned gesture, bends his countenance towards her, languid with the depth of his emotion. At her feet lie various instruments of music, broken and unstrung. Of the colouring I do not speak; it eclipses Nature, yet it has all her truth and softness.

We saw some pictures of Domenichino, Carracci, Albano, Guercino, Elisabetta Sirani. The two former—remember I do not pretend to taste —I cannot admire. Of the latter, there are some beautiful Madonnas. There are several of Guercino, which they said were very fine. I dare say they were, for the strength and complication of his figures made my head turn round. One, indeed, was certainly powerful. It was the representation of the founder of the Carthusians exercising his austerities in the desert, with a youth as his attendant, kneeling beside him at an altar; on another altar stood a skull and a crucifix; and around were the rocks and the trees of the wilderness. I never saw such a figure as this fellow. His face was wrinkled like a dried snake's skin, and drawn in long hard lines; his very hands were wrinkled. He looked like an animated mummy. He was clothed in a loose dress of death-coloured flannel, such as you might fancy a shroud might be after it had wrapt a corpse a month or two. It had a yellow, putrefied, ghastly hue, which it cast on all the objects around, so that the hands and face of the Carthusian and his companion were jaundiced by this sepulchral glimmer. Why write books against religion, when we may hang up such pictures? But the world either will not or cannot see. The gloomy effect of this was softened, and at the same time, its sublimity diminished, by the figure of the Virgin and child in the sky, looking down with admiration on the monk, and a beautiful flying figure of an angel.

Enough of pictures. I saw the place where Guido and his mistress, Elisabetta Sirani, were buried. This lady was poisoned at the age of twenty-six, by another lover, a rejected one, of course. Our guide said she was very ugly, and that we might see her portrait to-morrow.

Well, good-night for the present. "To-morrow to fresh fields and pastures new."

November 10.

To-day we first went to see those divine pictures of Raphael and Guido again, and then rode up the mountains, behind this city, to visit a chapel dedicated to the Madonna. It made me melancholy to see that they had been varnishing and restoring some of these pictures, and that even some had been pierced by French bayonets. These are the symptoms of the mortality of man ; and perhaps few of his works are more evanescent than paintings. Sculpture retains its freshness for twenty centuries. The Apollo and the Venus are as they were. But books are perhaps the only productions of man coeval with the human race. Sophocles and Shakespeare can be produced and reproduced for ever. But how evanescent are paintings, and must necessarily be! Those of Zeuxis and Apelles are no more, and perhaps they bore the same relation to Homer and Æschylus that those of Guido and Raphael bear to Dante and Petrarch. There is one refuge from the despondency of this contemplation. The material part, indeed, of their works must perish. But they survive in the mind of man, and the remembrances connected with them are transmitted from generation to generation. The poet embodies them in his creations. The systems of philosophers are modelled to gentleness by their contemplation; opinion, that legislator, is infected with their influence; men become better and wiser; and the unseen seeds are perhaps thus sown, which shall produce a plant more excellent even than that from which they fell. But all this might as well be said or thought at Marlow as Bologna. . . .

      Yours ever most sincerely,
            P. B. S.

XIX

To THOMAS LOVE PEACOCK.

Rome, 20 November, 1818.

MY DEAR PEACOCK,

Behold me in the capital of the vanished world! But I have seen nothing except St. Peter's and the Vatican, overlooking the city in the midst of distance, and the Dogana where they took us to have our luggage examined, which is built between the ruins of a temple to Antoninus Pius. The Corinthian columns rise over the dwindled palaces of the modern town, and the wrought cornice is changed on one side, as it were, to masses of wave-worn precipice, which overhang you, far, far on high.

I take the advantage of this rainy evening, and before Rome has effaced all other recollections, to endeavour to recall the vanished scenes through which we have passed. We left Bologna, I forget on what day, and passing by Rimini, Fano, and Foligno, along the Via Flaminia and Terni, have arrived at Rome after ten days' somewhat tedious, but most interesting journey. The most remarkable things we saw were the Roman excavations in the rock, and the great waterfall of

Terni. Of course you have heard that there are a Roman bridge and a triumphal arch at Rimini, and in what excellent taste they are built. The bridge is not unlike the Strand bridge, but more bold in proportion, and of course infinitely smaller. From Fano we left the coast of the Adriatic, and entered the Apennines, following the course of the Metaurus, the banks of which were the scene of the defeat of Asdrubal : and it is said, you can refer to the book, that Livy has given a very exact and animated description of it. I forget all about it, but shall look as soon as our boxes are opened. Following the river, the vale contracts, the banks of the river become steep and rocky, the forests of oak and ilex, which overhang its emerald-coloured stream, cling to their abrupt precipices. About four miles from Fossombrone, the river forces for itself a passage between the walls and toppling precipices of the loftiest Apennines, which are here rifted to their base, and undermined by the narrow and tumultuous torrent. It was a cloudy morning, and we had no conception of the scene that awaited us. Suddenly the low clouds were struck by the clear north wind, and like curtains of the finest gauze, removed one by one, were drawn from before the mountain, whose heaven-cleaving pinnacles and black crags overhanging one another stood at length defined in the light of day. The road runs parallel to the river, at a considerable height, and is carried through the mountain by a vaulted cavern. The marks of the chisel of the legionaries of the Roman consul are yet evident.

We passed on day after day, until we came to Spoleto, I think the most romantic city I ever saw. There is here an aqueduct of astonishing elevation, which unites two rocky mountains; there is a path of a torrent below, whitening the green dell with its broad and barren track of stones, and above there is a castle, apparently of great strength and tremendous magnitude, which overhangs the city, and whose marble bastions are perpendicular with the precipice. I never saw a more impressive picture, in which the shapes of nature are of the grandest order, but over which the creations of man, sublime from their antiquity and greatness, seem to predominate. The castle was built by Belisarius or Narses, I forget which, but was of that epoch.

From Spoleto we went to Terni, and saw the cataract of the Velino. The glaciers of Montanvert and the source of the Arveiron is the grandest spectacle I ever saw. This is the second. Imagine a river sixty feet in breadth, with a vast volume of waters, the outlet of a great lake among the higher mountains, falling 300 feet into a sightless gulf of snow-white vapour, which bursts up for ever and for ever from a circle of black crags, and thence leaping downwards, making five or six other cataracts, each fifty or a hundred feet high, which exhibit, on a smaller scale, and with beautiful and sublime variety, the same appearances. But words—and far less could painting—will not express it. Stand upon the brink of the platform of cliff which is directly opposite; you see the ever-moving water stream down. It comes in thick and tawny folds, flaking off like solid snow gliding down a mountain. It does not seem hollow within, but without it is unequal, like the folding of linen thrown carelessly down; your eye follows it, and it is lost below, not in the black rocks which gird it around, but in its own foam and spray in the cloudlike vapours boiling up from below, which is not like rain, nor mist, nor spray, nor foam, but water, in a shape wholly unlike anything I ever saw before. It is as white as snow, but thick and impenetrable to the eye. The very imagination is bewildered in it. A thunder comes up from the abyss wonderful to hear; for, though it ever sounds, it is never the same, but, modulated by the changing motion, rises and falls intermittingly; we passed half an hour in one spot looking at it, and thought but a few minutes had gone by. The surrounding scenery is in its kind the loveliest and most sublime that can be conceived. In our first walk we passed through some olive groves of large and ancient trees, whose hoary and twisted trunks leaned in all directions. We then crossed a path of orange trees by the riverside, laden with their golden fruit, and came to a forest of ilex of a large size, whose evergreen and acorn-bearing boughs were intertwined over our winding path. Around, hemming in the narrow vale, were pinnacles of lofty mountains of pyramidical rock clothed with all evergreen plants and trees; the vast pine, whose feathery foliage trembled in the blue air, the ilex, that ancestral inhabitant of these mountains, the arbutus with its crimson-coloured fruit and glittering leaves. After an hour's walk we came beneath the cataract of Terni, within the distance of half a mile; nearer you cannot approach, for the Nar, which has here its confluence with the Velino, bars the passage. We then crossed the river formed by this confluence, over a narrow natural bridge of rock, and saw the cataract from the platform I first mentioned. We think of spending some time next year near this waterfall. The inn is very bad, or we should have stayed there longer.

We came from Terni last night to a place called Nepi, and to-day arrived at Rome across the much belied Campagna di Roma, a place I confess infinitely to my taste. It is a flattering picture of Bagshot Heath, But then there are Apennines on one side and Rome and St. Peter's on the other, and it is intersected by perpetual dells clothed with arbutus and ilex. Adieu.

Very faithfully yours,
P. B. S.

XX

To THOMAS LOVE PEACOCK.

Naples, 22 December, 1818.

MY DEAR PEACOCK,

I have received a letter from you here, dated November 1st; you see the reciprocation of letters from the term of our travels is more slow. I entirely agree with what you say about "Childe Harold." The spirit in which it is written is, if insane, the most wicked and mischievous insanity that ever was given forth. It is a kind of obstinate and self-willed folly in which he hardens himself. I remonstrated with him in vain on the tone of mind from which such a view of things alone arises. For its real root is very different from its apparent one. Nothing can be less sublime than the true source of these expressions of contempt and desperation. The fact is that first, the Italian women with whom he associates are perhaps the most contemptible of all who exist under the moon, the most ignorant, the most disgusting, the most bigoted; countesses smell so strongly of garlic, that an ordinary Englishman cannot approach them. Well, L. B. is familiar with the lowest sort of these women, the people his gondolieri pick up in the streets. He associates with wretches who seem almost to have lost the gait and physiognomy of man, and who do not scruple to avow practices, which are not only not named, but I believe seldom even conceived in England. He says he disapproves, but he endures. He is heartily and deeply discontented with himself; and contemplating in the distorted mirror of his own thoughts the nature and the destiny of man, what can he behold but objects of contempt and despair? But that he is a great poet, I think the Address to Ocean proves. And he has a certain degree of candour while you talk to him, but unfortunately it does not outlast your departure. No, I do not doubt, and for his sake, I ought to hope, that his present career must end soon in some violent circumstance.

Since I last wrote to you, I have seen the ruins of Rome, the Vatican, St. Peter's, and all the miracles of ancient and modern art contained in that majestic city. The impression of it exceeds anything I have experienced in my travels. We stayed there only a week, intending to return at the end of February, and devote two or three months to its mines of inexhaustible contemplation, to which period I refer you for a minute account of it. We visited the Forum and the ruins of the Coliseum every day. The Coliseum is unlike any work of human hands I ever saw before. It is of enormous height and circuit, and arches built of massy stones are piled on one another, and jut into the blue air shattered into the forms of overhanging rocks. It has been changed by time into the image of an amphitheatre of rocky hills overgrown by the wild olive, the myrtle, and the fig-tree, and threaded by little paths which wind among its ruined stairs and immeasurable galleries : the copse-wood overshadows you as you wander through its labyrinths, and the wild weeds of this climate of flowers bloom under your feet. The arena is covered with grass, and pierces, like the skirts of a natural plain, the chasms of the broken arches around. But a small part of the exterior circumference remains; it is exquisitely light and beautiful, and the effect of the perfection of its architecture, adorned with ranges of Corinthian pilasters, supporting a bold cornice, is such as to diminish the effect of its greatness. The interior is all ruin. I can scarcely believe that when encrusted with Dorian marble and ornamented by columns of Egyptian granite, its effect could have been so sublime and so impressive as in its present state. It is open to the sky, and it was the clear and sunny weather of the end of

November in this climate when we visited it, day after day.

Near it is the Arch of Constantine, or rather the Arch of Trajan ; for the servile and avaricious senate of degraded Rome ordered that the monument of his predecessor should be demolished in order to dedicate one to the Christian reptile, who had crept among the blood of his murdered family to the supreme power. It is exquisitely beautiful and perfect. The Forum is a plain in the midst of Rome, a kind of desert full of heaps of stones and pits, and though so near the habitations of men, is the most desolate place you can conceive. The ruins of temples stand in and around it, shattered columns and ranges of others complete, supporting cornices of exquisite workmanship, and vast vaults of shattered domes distinct with regular compartments, once filled with sculptures of ivory or brass. The temples of Jupiter, and Concord, and Peace, and the Sun, and the Moon, and Vesta, are all within a short distance of this spot. Behold the wrecks of what a great nation once dedicated to the abstractions of the mind ! Rome is a city, as it were, of the dead, or rather of those who cannot die, and who survive the puny generations which inhabit and pass over the spot which they have made sacred to eternity. In Rome, at least in the first enthusiasm of your recognition of ancient time, you see nothing of the Italians. The nature of the city assists the delusion, for its vast and antique walls describe a circumference of sixteen miles, and thus the population is thinly scattered over this space, nearly as great as London. Wide wild fields are enclosed within it, and there are lanes and copses winding among the ruins, and a great green hill, lonely and bare, which overhangs the Tiber. The gardens of the modern palaces are like wild woods of cedar and cypress and pine, and the neglected walks are overgrown with weeds. The English burying place is a green slope near the walls, under the pyramidal tomb of Cestius, and is, I think, the most beautiful and solemn cemetery I ever beheld. To see the sun shining on its bright grass, fresh when we first visited it, with the autumnal dews, and hear the whispering of the wind among the leaves of the trees which have overgrown the tomb of Cestius, and the soil which is stirring in the sun-warm earth, and to mark the tombs, mostly of women and young people who were buried there, one might, if one were to die, desire the sleep they seem to sleep. Such is the human mind, and so it peoples with its wishes vacancy and oblivion.

I have told you little about Rome; but I reserve the Pantheon, and St. Peter's, and the Vatican, and Raphael, for my return. About a fortnight ago I left Rome, and Mary and Claire followed in three days, for it was necessary to procure lodgings here without alighting at an inn. From my peculiar mode of travelling I saw little of the country, but could just observe that the wild beauty of the scenery and the barbarous ferocity of the inhabitants progressively increased. On entering Naples, the first circumstance that engaged my attention was an assassination. A youth ran out of a shop, pursued by a woman with a bludgeon, and a man armed with a knife. The man overtook him, and with one blow in the neck laid him dead in the road. On my expressing the emotions of horror and indignation which I felt, a Calabrian priest, who travelled with me, laughed heartily, and attempted to quiz me, as what the English call a *flat*. I never felt such an inclination to beat any one. Heaven knows I have little power. But he saw that I looked extremely displeased, and was silent. This same man, a fellow of gigantic strength and stature, had expressed the most frantic terror of robbers on the road: he cried at the sight of my pistol, and it had been with great difficulty that the joint exertions of myself and the vetturino had quieted his hysterics.

But external nature in these delightful regions contrasts with and compensates for the deformity and degradation of humanity. We have a lodging divided from the sea by the Royal Gardens, and from our windows we see perpetually the blue waters of the bay, for ever changing, for ever the same, and encompassed by the mountainous island of Capreae, the lofty peaks which overhang Salerno, and the woody hill of Posilipo, whose promontories hide from us Misenum and the lofty isle Inarime, which, with its divided summit, forms the opposite horn of the bay. From the pleasant walks of the garden we see Vesuvius; a smoke by day and a fire by night is seen upon its summit, and the glassy sea often reflects its light or shadow. The climate is delicious. We sit without a fire, with the windows open, and have almost all the productions of an English summer. The weather is usually like what Wordsworth calls "the first fine day of March;" sometimes very much warmer, though perhaps it wants that "each minute sweeter than before," which gives an intoxicating sweetness to the awakening of the earth from its winter's sleep in England. We have made two excursions, one to Baiae, and one to

Vesuvius, and we propose to visit, successively, the islands, Paestum, Pompeii, and Beneventum.

We set off an hour after sunrise one radiant morning in a little boat ; there was not a cloud in the sky, nor a wave upon the sea, which was so translucent that you could see the hollow caverns clothed with the glaucous sea-moss, and the leaves and branches of those delicate weeds that pave the unequal bottom of the water. As noon approached, the heat, and especially the light, became intense. We passed Posilipo, and came first to the eastern point of the Bay of Puzzoli, which is within the great Bay of Naples, and which again encloses that of Baiae. Here are lofty rocks and craggy islets, with arches and portals of precipice standing in the sea, and enormous caverns, which echoed faintly with the murmur of the languid tide. This is called La Scuola di Virgilio. We then went directly across to the promontory of Misenum, leaving the precipitous island of Nisida on the right. Here we were conducted to see the Mare Morto, and the Elysian Fields ; the spot on which Virgil places the scenery of the sixth Aeneid. Though extremely beautiful, as a lake, and woody hills, and this divine sky must make it, I confess my disappointment. The guide showed us an antique cemetery, where the niches used for placing the cinerary urns of the dead yet remain. We then coasted the Bay of Baiae to the left, in which we saw many picturesque and interesting ruins; but I have to remark that we never disembarked but we were disappointed, while from the boat the effect of the scenery was inexpressibly delightful. The colours of the water and the air breathe over all things here the radiance of their own beauty. After passing the Bay of Baiae, and observing the ruins of its antique grandeur standing like rocks in the transparent sea under our boat, we landed to visit Lake Avernus. We passed through the cavern of the sibyl, not Virgil's sibyl, which pierces one of the hills which circumscribe the lake, and came to a calm and lovely basin of water surrounded by dark woody hills and profoundly solitary. Some vast ruins of the temple of Pluto stand on a lawny hill on one side of it, and are reflected in its windless mirror. It is far more beautiful than the Elysian Fields, but there are all the materials for beauty in the latter, and the Avernus was once a chasm of deadly and pestilential vapours. About half a mile from Avernus, a high hill called Monte Novo was thrown up by volcanic fire.

Passing onward we came to Pozzoli, the ancient Dicaearchea, where there are the columns remaining of a temple to Serapis, and the wreck of an enormous amphitheatre, changed, like the Coliseum, into a natural hill of the overteeming vegetation. Here also is the Solfatara, of which there is a poetical description in the " Civil War " of Petronius, beginning " Est locus," and in which the verses of the poet are infinitely finer than what he describes, for it is not a very curious place. After seeing these things we returned by moonlight to Naples in our boat. What colours there were in the sky, what radiance in the evening star, and how the moon was encompassed by a light unknown to our regions!

Our next excursion was to Vesuvius. We went to Resina in a carriage, where Mary and I mounted mules, and Claire was carried in a chair on the shoulders of four men, much like a member of Parliament after he has gained his election, and looking, with less reason, quite as frightened. So we arrived at the hermitage of San Salvador, where an old hermit, belted with rope, set forth the plates for our refreshment.

Vesuvius is, after the glaciers, the most impressive exhibition of the energies of nature I ever saw. It has not the immeasurable greatness, the overpowering magnificence, nor, above all, the radiant beauty of the glaciers; but it has all their character of tremendous and irresistible strength. From Resina to the hermitage you wind up the mountain, and cross a vast stream of hardened lava, which is an actual image of the waves of the sea, changed into hard block by enchantment. The lines of the boiling flood seem to hang in the air, and it is difficult to believe that the billows which seem hurrying down upon you are not actually in motion. This plain was once a sea of liquid fire. From the hermitage we crossed another vast stream of lava, and then went on foot up the cone. This is the only part of the ascent in which there is any difficulty, and that difficulty has been much exaggerated. It is composed of rocks of lava and declivities of ashes; by ascending the former, and descending the latter, there is very little fatigue. On the summit is a kind of irregular plain, the most horrible chaos that can be imagined; riven into ghastly chasms, and heaped up with tumuli of great stones and cinders, and enormous rocks blackened and calcined, which had been thrown from the volcano upon one another in terrible confusion. In the midst stands the conical hill, from which volumes of smoke and fountains of liquid fire, are rolled forth for ever. The mountain is at present in a slight state of eruption; and a thick heavy white smoke is perpetually rolled out, interrupted by enormous columns of an impenetrable black bituminous vapour, which is hurled up, fold after fold, into the sky with a deep hollow sound, and fiery stones are rained down from its darkness, and a black shower of ashes fell even where we sat. The lava, like the glacier, creeps on perpetually, with a crackling sound as of suppressed fire. There are several springs of lava; and in one place it gushes precipitously over a high crag, rolling down the half-molten rocks, and its own overhanging waves: a cataract of quivering fire. We approached the extremity of one of the rivers of lava; it is about twenty feet in breadth and ten in height; and as the inclined plane was not rapid, its motion was very slow. We saw the masses of its dark exterior surface detach themselves as it moved, and betray the depth of the liquid flame. In the day the fire is but slightly seen; you only observe a tremulous motion in the air, and streams and fountains of white sulphurous smoke.

At length we saw the sun sink between Capreae and Inarime, and, as the darkness increased, the effect of the fire became more beautiful. We were, as it were, surrounded by streams and cataracts of the red and radiant fire; and in the midst, from the column of bituminous smoke shot up into the air, fell the vast masses of rock, white with the light of their intense heat, leaving behind them through the dark vapour trains of splendour. We descended by torch-light, and I should have enjoyed the scenery on my return, but they conducted me, I know not how, to the hermitage in a state of intense bodily suffering, the worst effect of which was spoiling the pleasure of Mary and Claire. Our guides on the occasion were complete savages. You have no idea of the horrible cries which they suddenly utter, no one knows why, the clamour, the vociferation, the tumult. Claire in her palanquin suffered most from it; and when I had gone on before they threatened to leave her in the middle of the road, which they would have done had not my Italian servant promised them a beating, after which they became quiet. Nothing, however, can be more picturesque than the gestures and the physiognomies of these savage people. And when, in the darkness of night, they unexpectedly begin to sing in chorus some fragments of their wild but sweet national music, the effect is exceedingly fine.

Since I wrote this I have seen the Museum of this city. Such statues! There is a Venus; an ideal shape of the most winning loveliness. A Bacchus, more sublime than any living being. A

Satyr making love to a youth, in which the expressed life of the sculpture, and the inconceivable beauty of the form of the youth, overcome one's repugnance to the subject. There are multitudes of wonderfully fine statues found in Herculaneum and Pompeii. We are going to see Pompeii the first day that the sea is waveless. Herculaneum is almost filled up; no more excavations are made; the King bought the ground and built a palace upon it.

You don't see much of Hunt. I wish you could contrive to see him when you go to town, and ask him what he means to answer to Lord Byron's invitation. He has now an opportunity, if he likes, of seeing Italy. What do you think of joining his party, and paying us a visit next year; I mean as soon as the reign of winter is dissolved? Write to me your thoughts upon this. I cannot express to you the pleasure it would give me to welcome such a party.

I have depression enough of spirits and not good health, though I believe the warm air of Naples does me good. We see absolutely no one here.

   Adieu, my dear Peacock,
      Affectionately your friend,
         P. B. S.

XXI

To THOMAS LOVE PEACOCK.

Naples, 26 January, 1819.

MY DEAR PEACOCK,

Your two letters arrived within a few days of each other, one being directed to Naples, and the other to Livorno. They are more welcome visitors to me than mine can be to you—I writing as from sepulchres, you from the habitations of men yet unburied; though the sexton, Castlereagh, after having dug their grave, stands with his spade in his hand, evidently doubting whether he will not be forced to occupy it himself. Your news about the bank-note trials is excellent good. Do I not recognize in it the influence of Cobbett? You don't tell me what occupies Parliament? I know you will laugh at my demand, and assure me that it is indifferent. Your pamphlet I want exceedingly to see. Your calculations in the letter are clear, but require much oral explanation. You know I am an infernal arithmetician. If none but me had contemplated " lucentemque globum lunae, Titaniaque astra," the world would yet have doubted whether they were many hundred feet higher than the mountain tops.

In my accounts of pictures and things, I am more pleased to interest you than the many; and this is fortunate, because, in the first place I have no idea of attempting the latter, and if I did attempt it, I should assuredly fail. A perception of the beautiful characterizes those who differ from ordinary men, and those who can perceive it would not buy enough to pay the printer. Besides, I keep no journal, and the only records of my voyage will be letters I send to you. The bodily fatigue of standing for hours in galleries exhausts me: I believe that I don't see half what I ought, on that account. And then we know nobody, and the common Italians are so sullen and stupid, it's impossible to get information from them. At Rome, where the people seem superior to any in Italy, I cannot fail to stumble on something more. O, if I had health, and strength, and equal spirits, what boundless intellectual improvement might I not gather in this wonderful country! At present I write little else but poetry, and little of that. My first act of "Prometheus" is complete, and I think you would like it. I consider poetry very subordinate to moral and political science, and if I were well, certainly I would aspire to the latter, for I can conceive a great work, embodying the discoveries of all ages, and harmonizing the contending creeds by which mankind have been ruled. Far from me is such an attempt, and I shall be content, by exercising my fancy, to amuse myself, and perhaps some others, and cast what weight I can into the scale of that balance which the giant of Arthegall holds.

Since you last heard from me we have been to see Pompeii, and are waiting now for the return of spring weather, to visit, first, Paestum, and then the islands; after which we shall return to Rome. I was astonished at the remains of this city; I had no idea of anything so perfect yet remaining. My idea of the mode of its destruction was this:—First, an earthquake shattered it, and unroofed almost all its temples, and split its columns; then a rain of light, small pumice-stones fell; then torrents of boiling water, mixed with ashes, filled up all its crevices. A wide flat hill, from which the city was excavated, is now covered by thick woods, and you see the tombs and the theatres, the temples and the houses, surrounded by the uninhabited wilderness. We entered the town from the side towards the sea, and first saw two theatres, one more magnificent than the other, strewn with the ruins of the white marble which formed their seats and cornices, wrought with deep, bold sculpture. In the front, between the stage and the seats, is the circular space occasionally occupied by the chorus. The stage is very narrow, but long, and divided from this space by a narrow enclosure parallel to it, I suppose for the orchestra. On each side are the consuls' boxes, and below, in the theatre at Herculaneum, were found two equestrian statues of admirable workmanship, occupying the same place as the great bronze lamps did at Drury Lane. The smallest of the theatres is said to have been comic, though I should doubt. From both you see, as you sit on the seats, a prospect of the most wonderful beauty.

You then pass through the ancient streets; they are very narrow and the houses rather small, but all constructed on an admirable plan, especially for this climate. The rooms are built round a court, or sometimes two, according to the extent of the house. In the midst is a fountain, sometimes surrounded with a portico, supported on fluted columns of white stucco; the floor is paved with mosaic, sometimes wrought in imitation of vine leaves, sometimes in quaint figures, and more or less beautiful, according to the rank of the inhabitant. There were paintings on all, but most of them have been removed to decorate the royal museums. Little winged figures, and small orna-

ments of exquisite elegance yet remain. There is
an ideal life in the forms of these paintings of an
incomparable loveliness, though most are evidently
the work of very inferior artists. It seems as if, from
the atmosphere of mental beauty which surrounded
them, every human being caught a splendour not
his own. In one house you see how the bed-
rooms were managed;—a small sofa was built
up, where the cushions were placed; two pictures,
one representing Diana and Endymion, the other
Venus and Mars, decorate the chamber; and a
little niche, which contains the statue of a domestic
god. The floor is composed of a rich mosaic of
the rarest marbles, agate, jasper, and porphyry;
it looks to the marble fountain and the snow-white
columns, whose entablatures strew the floor of
the portico they supported. The houses have
only one story, and the apartments, though not
large, are very lofty. A great advantage results
from this, wholly unknown in our cities. The
public buildings, whose ruins are now forests as
it were of white fluted columns, and which then
supported entablatures loaded with sculptures,
were seen on all sides over the roofs of the houses.
This was the excellence of the ancients. Their
private expenses were comparatively moderate;
the dwelling of one of the chief senators of Pom-

peii is elegant indeed, and adorned with most beautiful specimens of art, but small. But their public buildings are everywhere marked by the bold and grand designs of an unsparing magnificence. In the little town of Pompeii—it contained about twenty thousand inhabitants—it is wonderful to see the number and the grandeur of their public buildings. Another advantage, too, is that, in the present case, the glorious scenery around is not shut out, and that, unlike the inhabitants of the Cimmerian ravines of modern cities, the ancient Pompeians could contemplate the clouds and the lamps of heaven; could see the moon rise high behind Vesuvius, and the sun set in the sea, tremulous with an atmosphere of golden vapour, between Inarime and Misenum.

We next saw the temples. Of the temple of Aesculapius little remains but an altar of black stone, adorned with a cornice imitating the scales of a serpent. His statue, in terra-cotta, was found in the cell. The temple of Isis is more perfect. It is surrounded by a portico of fluted columns, and in the area around it are two altars, and many ceppi for statues; and a little chapel of white stucco, as hard as stone, of the most exquisite proportion; its panels are adorned with figures in bas-relief, slightly indicated, but of a workmanship the most delicate and perfect that can be conceived. They are Egyptian subjects, executed by a Greek artist, who has harmonised all the unnatural extravagances of the original conception into the supernatural loveliness of his country's genius. They scarcely touch the ground with their feet, and their wind-uplifted robes seem in the place of wings. The temple in the midst, raised on a high platform, and approached by steps, was decorated with exquisite paintings, some of which we saw in the museum at Portici. It is small, of the same materials as the chapel, with a pavement of mosaic and fluted Ionic columns of white stucco, so white that it dazzles you to look at it.

Thence through other porticos and labyrinths of walls and columns, for I cannot hope to detail everything to you, we came to the Forum. This is a large square surrounded by lofty porticos of fluted columns, some broken, some entire, their entablatures strewed under them. The temple of Jupiter, of Venus, and another temple, the tribunal, and the hall of public justice, with their forests of lofty columns, surround the Forum. Two pedestals or altars of an enormous size—for, whether they supported equestrian statues, or were the altars of the temple of Venus, before which they stand, the guide could not tell—occupy the lower end of the Forum. At the upper end, supported on an elevated platform, stands the temple of Jupiter. Under the colonnade of its portico we sate, and pulled out our oranges, and figs, and bread, and medlars—sorry fare, you will say—and rested to eat. Here was a magnificent spectacle. Above and between the multitudinous shafts of the sunshining columns was seen the sea, reflecting the purple heaven of noon above it, and supporting, as it were, on its line the dark lofty mountains of Sorrento, of a blue inexpressibly deep, and tinged towards their summits with streaks of new-fallen snow. Between was one small green island. To the right was Capreae, Inarime, Prochyta, and Misenum. Behind was the single summit of Vesuvius, rolling forth volumes of thick white smoke, whose foam-like column was sometimes darted into the clear dark sky, and fell in little streaks along the wind. Between Vesuvius and the nearer mountains, as through a chasm, was seen the main line of the loftiest Apennines to the east. The day was radiant and warm. Every now and then we heard subterranean thunder of Vesuvius; its distant deep peals seemed to shake the very air and light of day, which interpenetrated our frames, with the sullen and tremendous sound. This scene was what the Greeks beheld; Pompeii, you know, was a Greek city. They lived in harmony with nature; and the interstices of their incomparable columns were portals, as it were, to admit the spirit of beauty which animates this glorious universe to visit those whom it inspired. If such was Pompeii, what was Athens? What scene was exhibited from the Acropolis, the Parthenon, and the temples of Hercules, and Theseus, and the Winds? the islands and the Aegean sea, the mountains of Argolis, and the peaks of Pindus and Olympus, and the darkness of the Boeotian forests interspersed?

From the Forum we went to another public place; a triangular portico, half inclosing the ruins of an enormous temple. It is built on the edge of the hill overlooking the sea. That black point is the temple. In the apex of the triangle stands an altar and a fountain, and before the altar once stood the statue of the builder of the portico. Returning hence, and following the consular road, we came to the eastern gate of the city. The walls are of enormous strength and inclose a space of three miles. On each side of the road beyond the gate are built the tombs. How unlike ours! They seem not so much hiding places of that which must decay, as voluptuous chambers for immortal spirits. They are of marble, radiantly white; and two, especially beautiful, are loaded with exquisite bas-reliefs. On the stucco-wall that incloses them are little emblematic figures of a relief exceedingly low, of dead and dying animals, and little winged genii, and female forms bending in groups in some funeral office. The higher reliefs represent, one a nautical subject, and the other a bacchanalian one. Within the cell stand the cinerary urns, sometimes one, sometimes more. It is said that paintings were found within; which are now, as has been everything moveable in Pompeii, removed, and scattered about in royal museums. These tombs were the most impressive things of all. The wild woods surround them on either side; and along the broad stones of the paved road which divided them, you hear the late leaves of autumn shiver and rustle in the stream of the inconstant wind, as it were, like the step of ghosts. The radiance and magnificence of these dwellings of the dead, the white freshness of the scarcely finished marble, the impassioned or imaginative life of the figures which adorn them, contrast strangely with the simplicity of the houses of those who were living when Vesuvius overwhelmed them.

I have forgotten the amphitheatre, which is of great magnitude, though much inferior to the Coliseum. I now understand why the Greeks were such great poets: and, above all, I can account, it seems to me, for the harmony, the unity, the perfection, the uniform excellence, of all their works of art. They lived in a perpetual commerce with external nature, and nourished themselves upon its forms. Their theatres were all open to the mountains and the sky. Their columns, the ideal types of a sacred forest, with its roof of interwoven tracery, admitted the light and wind; the odour and the freshness of the country penetrated the cities. Their temples were mostly upaithric; and the flying clouds, the stars, or the deep sky, were seen above. O, but for that series of wretched wars which terminated in the Roman conquest of the world ; but for the Christian religion, which put the finishing stroke on the ancient system ; but for those changes that conducted Athens to its ruin,—to what an eminence might not humanity have arrived !

    Adieu ! yours most faithfully,
            P. B. S.

XXII

To Thomas Love Peacock.

Naples, 25 February, 1819.

MY DEAR PEACOCK,

I am much interested to hear of your progress in the object of your removal to London, especially as I hear from Horace Smith of the advantages attending it. There is no person in the world who would more sincerely rejoice in any good fortune that might befall you than I should.

We are on the point of quitting Naples for Rome. The scenery which surrounds this city is more delightful than any within the immediate reach of civilized man. I don't think I have mentioned to you the Lago d'Agnano and the Caccia d'Ischieri, and I have since seen what obscures those lovely forms in my memory. They are both the craters of extinguished volcanos, and nature has thrown forth forests of oak and ilex, and spread mossy lawns and clear lakes over the dead or sleeping fire. The first is a scene of a wider and milder character, with soft sloping, wooded hills, and grassy declivities declining to the lake, and cultivated plains of vines woven upon poplar-trees, bounded by the theatre of hills. Innumerable wild water-birds, quite tame, inhabit this place. The other is a royal chace, is surrounded by steep and lofty hills, and only accessible through a wide gate of massy oak, from the vestibule of which the spectacle of precipitous hills, hemming in a narrow and circular vale, is suddenly disclosed. The hills are covered with thick woods of ilex, myrtle, and laurustinus; the polished leaves of the ilex, as they wave in their multitudes under the partial blasts which rush through the chasms of the vale, glitter above the dark masses of foliage below, like the white foam of waves upon the deep blue sea. The plain so surrounded is at most three miles in circumference. It is occupied partly by a lake, with bold shores wooded by evergreens, and interrupted by a sylvan promontory of the wild forest whose mossy boughs overhang its expanse, of a silent and purple darkness, like an Italian midnight; and partly by the forest itself, of all gigantic trees, but the oak especially, whose jagged boughs, now leafless, are hoary with thick lichens, and loaded with the massy and deep foliage of the ivy. The effect of the dark eminences that surround this plain, seen through the boughs, is of an enchanting solemnity. There we saw in one instance wild boars and a deer, and in another, a spectacle little suited to the antique and Latonian nature of the place—King Ferdinand in a winter enclosure, watching to shoot wild boars. The underwood was principally evergreen, all lovely kinds of fern and furze; the cytisus, a delicate kind of furze, with a pretty yellow blossom, the myrtle, and the myrica. The willow-trees had just begun to put forth their green and golden buds, and gleamed like points of lambent fire along the wintry forest. The Grotto del Cane, too, we saw, because other people see it; but would not allow the dog to be exhibited in torture for our curiosity. The poor little animals stood moving their tails in a slow and dismal manner, as if perfectly resigned to their condition, a cur-like emblem of voluntary servitude. The effect of the vapour, which extinguishes a torch, is to cause suffocation at last, through a process which makes the lungs feel as if they were torn by sharp points within. So a surgeon told us, who tried the experiment on himself.

There was a Greek city, sixty miles to the south of Naples, called Posidonia, now Pesto, where there still subsist three temples of Etruscan architecture, still perfect. From this city we have just returned. The weather was most unfavourable for our expedition. After two months of cloudless serenity, it began raining cats and dogs. The first night we slept at Salerno, a large city situate in the recess of a deep bay; surrounded with stupendous mountains of the same name. A few miles from Torre del Greco we entered on the pass of the mountains, which is a line dividing the isthmus of those enormous piles of rock which compose the southern boundary of the Bay of Naples, and the northern one of that of Salerno. On one side is a lofty conical hill, crowned with the turrets of a ruined castle, and out into platforms for cultivation—at least every ravine and glen, whose precipitous sides admitted of other vegetation but that of the rock-rooted ilex: on the other the aetherial snowy crags of an immense mountain, whose terrible lineaments were at intervals concealed or disclosed by volumes of dense clouds rolling under the tempest. Half a mile from this spot, between orange and lemon groves of a lovely village, suspended as it were on an amphitheatral precipice, whose golden globes contrasted with the white walls and dark green leaves which they almost outnumbered, shone the sea. A burst of the declining sunlight illumined it. The road led along the brink of the precipice, towards Salerno. Nothing could be more glorious than the scene. The immense mountains covered with the rare and divine vegetation of this climate, with many-folding vales, and deep dark recesses, which the fancy scarcely could penetrate, descended from their snowy summits precipitously to the sea. Before us was Salerno, built into a declining plain, between the mountains and the sea. Beyond, the other shore of sky-cleaving mountains, then dim with the mist of tempest. Underneath, from the base of the precipice where the road conducted, rocky promontories jutted into the sea, covered with olive and ilex woods, or with the ruined battlements of some Roman or Saracenic fortress. We slept at Salerno, and the next morning, before daybreak, proceeded to Posidonia. The night had been tempestuous, and our way lay by the sea sand. It was utterly dark, except when the long line of wave burst, with a sound like thunder, beneath the starless sky, and cast up a kind of mist of cold white lustre. When morning came, we found ourselves travelling in a wide desert plain, perpetually interrupted by wild irregular glens, and bounded on all sides by the Apennines and the sea. Sometimes it was covered with forest, sometimes dotted with underwood, or mere tufts of fern and furze, and the wintry dry tendrils of creeping plants. I have never, but in the Alps, seen an amphitheatre of mountains so magnificent. After travelling fifteen miles, we came to a river, the bridge of which had been broken, and which was so swollen that the ferry would not take the carriage across. We had, therefore, to walk seven miles of a muddy road, which led to the ancient city across the desolate Maremma. The air was scented with the sweet smell of violets of an extraordinary size and beauty. At length we saw the sublime and massy colonnades, skirting the horizon of the wilderness. We entered by the ancient gate, which is now no more than a chasm in the rock-like wall. Deeply sunk in the ground beside it were the ruins of a sepulchre, which the ancients were in the habit of building beside the public way. The first temple, which is the smallest, consists of an outer range of columns, quite perfect, and supporting a perfect architrave and two shattered frontispieces. The proportions are extremely massy, and the architecture entirely unornamented and simple. These columns do not seem more than forty feet high, but the perfect proportions diminish the apprehension of their magnitude; it seems as if inequality and irregularity of form were requisite to force on us the relative idea of greatness. The scene from between the columns of the temple consists on one side of the sea, to which the gentler hill on which it is built slopes; and on the other of the grand amphitheatre of the loftiest Apennines, dark purple mountains, crowned with snow, and intersected here and there by long bars of hard and leaden-coloured cloud. The effect of the jagged outline of mountains, through groups of enormous columns on one side, and on the other the level horizon of the sea, is inexpressibly grand. The second temple is much larger, and also more perfect. Beside the outer range of columns, it contains an interior range of column above column, and the ruins of a wall which was the screen of the Penetralia. With little diversity of ornament, the order of architecture is similar to that of the first temple. The columns in all are fluted, and built of a porous volcanic stone, which time has dyed with a rich and yellow colour. The columns are one-third larger, and, like that of the first, diminish from the base to the capital, so that, but for the chastening effect of their admirable proportions, their magnitude would, from the delusion of perspective, seem greater, not less, than it is: though perhaps we ought to say, not that this symmetry diminishes your apprehension of their magnitude, but that it overpowers the idea of relative greatness, by establishing within itself a system of relations destructive of your idea of its relation with other objects, on which our ideas of size depend. The third temple is what they call a basilica; three columns alone remain of the interior range ; the exterior is perfect, but that the cornice and frieze in many places have fallen. This temple covers more ground than either of the others, but its columns are of an intermediate magnitude between those of the second and the first.

We only contemplated these sublime monuments for two hours, and of course could only bring away so imperfect a conception of them as is the shadow of some half-remembered dream.

The royal collection of paintings in this city is sufficiently miserable. Perhaps the most remarkable is the original studio by Michael Angelo, of the " Day of Judgment," which is painted in fresco on the Sixtine Chapel of the Vatican. It is there so defaced as to be wholly indistinguishable. I cannot but think the genius of this artist overrated. He has not only no temperance, no modesty, no feeling for the just boundaries of art— and in these respects any admirable genius may err—but has no sense of beauty, and to want this is to want the sense of the creative power of mind. What is terror without a contrast with, and a connexion with, loveliness? How well

Dante understood this secret, Dante, with whom this artist has been so presumptuously compared! What a thing his "Moses" is; how distorted from all that is natural and majestic, only less monstrous and detestable than its historical prototype. In the picture to which I allude, God is leaning out of heaven, as it were eagerly enjoying the final scene of the infernal tragedy He set the universe to act. The Holy Ghost, in the shape of a dove, is under him. Under the Holy Ghost stands Jesus Christ, in an attitude of haranguing the assembly. This figure, which his subject, or rather the view which it became him to take of it, ought to have modelled of a calm, severe, awe-inspiring majesty, terrible, yet lovely, is in the attitude of a commonplace resentment. On one side of this figure are the elect; on the other, the host of heaven; they ought to have been what the Christians called glorified bodies, floating onwards with that everlasting light (I speak in the spirit of their faith) which had consumed their mortal veil. They are in fact very ordinary people. Below is the ideal purgatory, I imagine, in mid-air, in the shape of spirits, some of whom demons are dragging down, others falling as it were by their own weight, others half suspended in that Mahomet-coffin kind of attitude which most moderate

Christians, I believe, expect to assume. Every step towards hell approximates to the region of the artist's exclusive power. There is great imagination in many of the situations of these unfortunate spirits. But hell and death are his real sphere. The bottom of the picture is divided by a lofty rock, in which there is a cavern whose entrance is thronged by devils, some coming in with spirits, some going out for prey. The blood-red light of the fiery abyss glows through their dark forms. On one side are the devils in all hideous forms, struggling with the damned, who have received their sentence at the Redeemer's throne, and chained in all forms of agony by knotted serpents, and writhing on the crags in all variety of torture. On the other, are the dead coming out of their graves, horrible forms. Such is the famous "Day of Judgment" of Michael Angelo; a kind of "Titus Andronicus" in painting, but the author surely no Shakspeare. The other paintings are one or two of Raphael or his pupils, very sweet and lovely : a "Danae," of Titian, a picture, the softest and most voluptuous form, with languid and uplifted eyes, and warm yet passive limbs ; a "Maddalena," by Guido, with dark-brown hair, and dark-brown eyes, and an earnest, soft, melancholy look ; and some excellent pictures, in point of execution, by Annibal Carracci. None others worth a second look. Of the gallery of statues I cannot speak. They require a volume, not a letter. Still less, what can I do at Rome?

Most faithfully yours,
P. B. S.

XXIII

To THOMAS LOVE PEACOCK.

Rome, 23rd March 1819.

MY DEAR PEACOCK,

I wrote to you the day before our departure from Naples. We came by slow journeys, with our own horses, to Rome, resting one day at Mola di Gaeta, at the inn called Villa di Cicerone, from being built on the ruins of his villa, whose immense substructions overhang the sea, and are scattered among the orange-groves. Nothing can be lovelier than the scene from the terraces of the inn. On one side precipitous mountains, whose bases slope into an inclined plane of olive and orange-copses, the latter forming, as it were, an emerald sky of leaves, starred with innumerable globes of their ripening fruit, whose rich splendour contrasted with the deep green foliage; on the other the sea, bounded on one side by the antique town of Gaeta, and on the other by what appears to be an island, the promontory of Circe. From Gaeta to Terracina the whole scenery is of the most sublime character. At Terracina precipitous conical crags of immense height shoot into the sky and overhang the sea. At Albano we arrived again in sight of Rome. Arches after arches in unending lines stretching across the uninhabited wilderness, the blue defined lines of the mountains seen between them; masses of nameless ruin standing like rocks out of the plain; and the plain itself, with its billowy and unequal surface, announced the neighbourhood of Rome. And what shall I say to you about Rome? If I speak of the inanimate ruins, the rude stones piled upon stones, which are the sepulchres of the fame of those who once arrayed them with the beauty which has faded, will you believe me insensible to the vital, the almost breathing creations of genius yet subsisting in their perfection? What has become, you will ask, of the Apollo, the Gladiator, or the Venus of the Capitol? What of the Apollo di Belvedere, the Laocoon? What of Raphael and Guido? These things are best spoken of when the mind has drunk in the spirit of their forms; and little indeed can I, who must devote no more than a few months to the contemplation of them, hope to know or feel of their profound beauty?

I think I told you of the Coliseum, and its impressions on me on my first visit to this city. The next most considerable relic of antiquity, considered as a ruin, is the Thermæ of Caracalla. These consist of six enormous chambers, above 200 feet in height, and each inclosing a vast space like that of a field. There are, in addition, a number of towers and labyrinthine recesses, hidden and woven over by the wild growth of weeds and ivy. Never was any desolation more sublime and lovely. The perpendicular wall of ruin is cloven into steep ravines filled up with flowering shrubs, whose thick twisted roots are knotted in the rifts of the stones. At every step the aerial pinnacles of shattered stone group into new combinations of effect, and tower above the lofty yet level walls, as the distant mountains change their aspect to one travelling rapidly along the plain. The perpendicular walls resemble nothing more than that cliff of Bisham Wood, that is overgrown with wood, and yet is stony and precipitous. You know the one I mean; not the chalk-pit, but the spot that has the pretty copse of fir-trees and privet-bushes at its base, and where Hogg and I scrambled up, and you, to my infinite discontent, would go home. These walls surround green and level spaces of lawn, on which some elms have grown, and which are interspersed towards their skirts by masses of the fallen ruin, overtwined with the broad leaves of the creeping weeds. The blue sky canopies it, and is as the everlasting roof of these enormous halls.

But the most interesting effect remains. In one of the buttresses, that supports an immense and lofty arch, which " bridges the very winds of heaven," are the crumbling remains of an antique winding staircase, whose sides are open in many places to the precipice. This you ascend, and arrive on the summit of these piles. There grow on every side thick entangled wildernesses of myrtle, and the myrletus, and bay, and the flowering laurustinus, whose white blossoms are just developed, the wild fig, and a thousand nameless plants sown by the wandering winds; these woods are intersected on every side by paths, like sheep-tracks through the copse-wood of steep mountains, which wind to every part of the immense labyrinth. From the midst rise those pinnacles and masses, themselves like mountains, which have been seen from below. In one place you wind along a narrow strip of weed-grown ruin, on one side is the immensity of earth and sky, on the other a narrow chasm, which is bounded by an arch of enormous size, fringed by the many-coloured foliage and blossoms, and supporting a lofty and irregular pyramid, overgrown like itself with the all-prevailing vegetation. Around arise other crags and other peaks, all arrayed, and the deformity of their vast desolation softened down, by the undecaying investiture of nature. Come to Rome. It is a scene by which expression is overpowered; which words cannot convey. Still further, winding up one half of the shattered pyramids, by the path through the blooming copse-wood, you come to a little mossy lawn, surrounded by the wild shrubs; it is overgrown with anemones, wall-flowers, and violets, whose stalks pierce the starry moss, and with radiant blue flowers, whose names I know not, and which scatter through the air the divinest odour, which, as you recline under the shade of the ruin, produces sensations of voluptuous faintness, like the combinations of sweet music. The paths still wind on, threading the perplexed windings, other labyrinths, other lawns, and deep dells of wood, and lofty rocks, and terrific chasms. When I tell you that these ruins cover several acres, and that the paths above penetrate at least half their extent, your imagination will fill up all that I am unable to express of this astonishing scene.

I speak of these things not in the order in which I visited them, but in that of the impression which they made on me, or perhaps chance directs. The ruins of the ancient Forum are so far fortunate that they have not been walled up in the modern city. They stand in an open, lonesome place, bounded on one side by the modern city, and the other by the Palatine Mount, covered with shapeless masses of ruin. The tourists tell you all about these things, and I am afraid of stumbling on their language when I enumerate what is so well known. There remain eight granite columns of the Ionic order, with the entablature of the Temple of Concord, founded by Camillus. I fear that the immense expense demanded by these columns forbids us to hope that they are the remains of any edifice dedicated by that most perfect and virtuous of men. It is supposed to have been repaired under the Eastern emperors; alas, what a contrast of recollections! Near them stand three Corinthian fluted columns, which supported the angle of a temple; the architrave and entablature are worked with delicate sculpture. Beyond, to the south, is another solitary column; and still more distant, three more, supporting the wreck of an entablature. Descending from the Capitol to the Forum, is the triumphal arch of Septimus Severus, less perfect than that of Constantine, though from its proportions and magnitude a most impressive monument. That of Constantine, or rather of Titus—for the relief and sculpture, and even the colossal images of Dacian captives, were torn by a decree of the Senate from an arch dedicated to the latter, to adorn that of this stupid and wicked monster, Constantine, one of whose chief merits consists in establishing a religion, the destroyer of those arts which would have rendered so base a spoliation unnecessary—is the most perfect. It is an admirable work of art. It is built of the finest marble, and the outline of the reliefs is in many parts as perfect as if just finished. Four Corinthian fluted columns support, on each side, a bold entablature, whose bases are loaded with reliefs of captives in every attitude of humiliation and slavery. The compartments above express in bolder relief the enjoyment of success—the conqueror on his throne or in his chariot, or nodding over the crushed multitudes, who writhe under his horses' hoofs—as those below express the torture and abjectness of defeat. There are three arches whose roofs are panelled with fretwork, and their sides adorned with similar reliefs. The keystone of these arches is supported each by two winged figures of Victory, whose hair floats on the wind of their own speed, and whose arms are outstretched, bearing trophies, as if impatient to meet. They look, as it were, borne from the subject extremities of the earth, on the breath which is the exhalation of that battle and desolation, which it is their mission to commemorate. Never were monuments so completely fitted to the purpose for which they were designed, of expressing that mixture of energy and error which is called a triumph.

I walk forth in the purple and golden light of an Italian evening, and return by starlight or moonlight, through this scene. The elms are just budding, and the warm spring winds bring unknown odours, all sweet, from the country. I see the radiant Orion through the mighty columns of the Temple of Concord, and the mellow fading light softens down the modern buildings of the Capitol, the only ones that interfere with the sublime desolation of the scene. On the steps of the Capitol itself, stand two colossal statues of Castor and Pollux, each with his horse, finely executed, though far inferior to those of Monte Cavallo, the cast of one of which you know we saw together in London. This walk is close to our lodging, and this is my evening walk.

What shall I say of the modern city? Rome is yet the capital of the world. It is a city of palaces and temples more glorious than those which any other city contains, and of ruins more glorious than they. Seen from any of the eminences that surround it, it exhibits domes beyond domes, and palaces, and colonnades interminably, even to the horizon; interspersed with patches of desert, and mighty ruins which stand girt by their own desolation, in the midst of the fanes of living religions, and the habitations of living men, in sublime loneliness. St. Peter's is, as you have heard, the loftiest building in Europe. Externally it is inferior in architectural beauty to St. Paul's, though not wholly devoid of it; internally it exhibits littleness on a large scale, and is in every respect opposed to antique taste. You know my propensity to admire; and I tried to persuade myself out of this opinion, in vain; the more I see of the interior of St. Peter's the less impression as a whole does it produce on me. I cannot even think it lofty, though its dome is considerably higher than any hill within fifty miles of London; and when one reflects, it is an astonishing monument of the daring energy of man. Its colonnade is wonderfully fine, and there are two fountains, which rise in spire-like columns of water to an immense height in the sky, and falling on the porphyry vases from which they spring, fill the whole air with a radiant mist, which at noon is thronged with innumerable rainbows. In the midst stands an obelisk. In front is the palace-like façade of St. Peter's, certainly magnificent; and there is produced on the whole, an architectural combination unequalled in the world. But the dome of the temple is concealed, except at a very great distance, by the façade and the inferior part of the building, and that diabolical contrivance they call an attic.

The effect of the Pantheon is totally the reverse of that of St. Peter's. Though not a fourth part of the size, it is, as it were, the visible image of the universe; in the perfection of its proportions, as when you regard the unmeasured dome of heaven, the idea of magnitude is swallowed up and lost. It is open to the sky, and its wide dome is lighted by the ever-changing illumination of the air. The clouds of noon fly over it, and at night the keen stars are seen through the azure darkness, hanging immoveably, or driving after the driving moon among the clouds. We visited it by moonlight; it is supported by sixteen columns, fluted and Corinthian, of a certain rare and beautiful yellow marble, exquisitely polished, called here Giallo Antico. Above these are the niches for the statues of the twelve gods.

This is the only defect of this sublime temple; there ought to have been no interval between the commencement of the dome and the cornice, supported by the columns. Thus there would have been no diversion from the magnificent simplicity of its form. This improvement is alone wanting to have completed the unity of the idea.

The fountains of Rome are, in themselves, magnificent combinations of art, such as alone it were worth coming to see. That in the Piazza Navona, a large square, is composed of enormous fragments of rock, piled on each other, and penetrated as by caverns. This mass supports an Egyptian obelisk of immense height; on the four corners of the rock recline, in different attitudes, colossal figures representing the four divisions of the globe. The water bursts from the crevices beneath them. They are sculptured with great spirit; one impatiently tearing a veil from his eyes; another with his hands stretched upwards. The Fontana di Trevi is the most celebrated, and is rather a waterfall than a fountain; gushing out from masses of rock, with a gigantic figure of Neptune; and below are two river gods, checking two winged horses, struggling up from among the rocks and waters. The whole is not ill-conceived nor executed; but you know not how delicate the imagination becomes by dieting with antiquity day after day. The only things that sustain the comparison are Raphael, Guido, and Salvator Rosa.

The fountain on the Quirinal, or rather the group formed by the statues, obelisk, and the fountain, is, however, the most admirable of all. From the Piazza Quirinale, or rather Monte Cavallo, you see the boundless ocean of domes, spires, and columns which is the city Rome. On a pedestal of white marble rises an obelisk of red granite, piercing the blue sky. Before it is a vast basin of porphyry, in the midst of which rises a column of the purest water, which collects into itself all the overhanging colours of the sky, and breaks them into a thousand prismatic hues and graduated shadows; they fall together with its dashing water-drops into the outer basin. The elevated situation of this basin produces, I imagine, this effect of colour on each side. On an elevated pedestal stand the statues of Castor and Pollux, each in the act of taming his horse, which are said, but I believe wholly without authority, to be the work of Phidias and Praxiteles. These figures combine the irresistible energy with the sublime and the perfect loveliness supposed to have belonged to their divine nature. The reins no longer exist, but the position of their hands and the sustained and calm command of their regard seem to require no mechanical aid to enforce obedience. The countenances at so great a height are scarcely visible, and I have a better idea of that of which we saw a cast together in London, than of the other. But the sublime and living majesty of their limbs and mien, the nervous and fiery animation of the horses they restrain, seen in the blue sky of Italy, and overlooking the city of Rome, surrounded by the light and the music of that crystalline fountain, no cast can communicate.

These figures were found at the Baths of Constantine, but, of course, are of remote antiquity. I do not acquiesce however in the practice of attributing to Phidias, or Praxiteles, or Scopas, or some great master, any admirable work that may be found. We find little of what remained, and perhaps the works of these were such as greatly surpassed all that we conceive of most perfect and admirable in what little has escaped the deluge. If I am too jealous of the honour of the Greeks, our masters and creators, the gods whom we should worship, pardon me.

I have said what I feel without entering into any critical discussions of the ruins of Rome, and the mere outside of this inexhaustible mine of thought and feeling. Hobhouse, Eustace, and Forsyth will tell all the shew-knowledge about it, "the common stuff of the earth." By-the-bye, Forsyth is worth reading as I judge from a chapter or two I have seen. I cannot get the book here.

I ought to have observed that the central arch of the triumphal arch of Titus yet subsists, more perfect in its proportions, they say, than any of a later date. This I did not remark. The figures of Victory, with unfolded wings, and each spurning back a globe with outstretched feet, are, perhaps, more beautiful than those on either of the others. Their lips are parted: a delicate mode of indicating the fervour of their desire to arrive at the destined resting-place, and to express the eager respiration of their speed. Indeed, so essential to beauty were the forms expressive of the exercise of the imagination and the affections considered by Greek artists, that no ideal figure of antiquity, not destined to some representation directly exclusive of such a character, is to be found with closed lips. Within this arch are two panelled alto relievos, one representing a train of

people bearing in procession the instruments of
Jewish worship, among which is the holy candle-
stick with seven branches; on the other, Titus
standing in a quadriga, with a winged Victory.
The grouping of the horses, and the beauty,
correctness, and energy of their delineation, is
remarkable, though they are much destroyed.

P. B. S.

XXIV

To Leigh Hunt.

Livorno, 27th Sept. 1819.

MY DEAR FRIEND,

We are now on the point of leaving this place for Florence, where we have taken pleasant apartments for six months, which brings us to the 1st of April; the season at which new flowers and new thoughts spring forth upon the earth and in the mind. What is then our destination is yet undecided. I have not yet seen Florence, except as one sees the outside of the streets; but its physiognomy indicates it to be a city, which, though the ghost of a republic, yet possesses most amiable qualities. I wish you could meet us there in the spring, and we would try to muster up a "Lieta Brigata," which leaving behind them the pestilence of remembered misfortunes, might act over again the pleasures of the interlocutors in Boccaccio. I have been lately reading this most divine writer. He is in a high sense of the word a poet, and his language has the rhythm and harmony of verse. I think him not equal certainly either to Dante or Petrarch, but far superior to Tasso and Ariosto, the children

of a later and of a colder day. I consider the three
first as the productions of the vigour of the
infancy of a new nation, as rivulets from the
same spring as that which fed the greatness of
the republics of Florence and Pisa, and which
checked the influence of the German Emperors;
and from which, through obscurer channels,
Raphael and Michael Angelo drew the light and
the harmony of their inspiration. When the
second-rate poets of Italy wrote, the corrupting
blight of tyranny was already hanging on every
bud of genius. Energy and simplicity and unity
of idea were no more. In vain do we seek in the
finest passages of Ariosto and Tasso, any expression which at all approaches in this respect to
those of Dante and Petrarch. How much do I
admire Boccaccio! What descriptions of nature
are those in his little introductions to every new
day! It is the morning of life, stripped of that
mist of familiarity which makes it obscure to us.
Boccaccio seems to me to have possessed a deep
sense of the fair ideal of human life, considered
in its social relations. His more serious theories
of love agree especially with mine. He often
expresses things lightly too, which have serious
meanings of a very beautiful kind. He is a
moral casuist, the opposite of the Christian,

stoical, ready-made, and worldly system of morals. Do you remember one little remark, or rather maxim of his, which might do some good to the common narrow-minded conceptions of love, "Bocca baciata non perde ventura; anzi rinnuova, come fa la luna?"

We expect Mary to be confined towards the end of October. The birth of a child will probably retrieve her from some part of her present melancholy depression.

It would give me much pleasure to know Mr. Lloyd. Do you know, when I was in Cumberland, I got Southey to borrow a copy of Berkeley from him, and I remember observing some pencil notes in it, probably written by Lloyd, which I thought particularly acute. One, especially, struck me as being the assertion of a doctrine, of which even then I had long been persuaded, and on which I had founded much of my persuasions, as regarded the imagined cause of the universe, "Mind cannot create, it can only perceive." Ask him if he remembers having written it. Of Lamb you know my opinion, and you can bear witness to the regret which I felt, when I learned that the calumny of an enemy had deprived me of his society whilst in England. Ollier told me that the "Quarterly" are going to review me. I suppose it will be a pretty . . ., and as I am acquiring a taste for humour and drollery, I confess I am curious to see it. I have sent my "Prometheus Unbound" to Peacock; if you ask him for it he will show it you. I think it will please you.

Whilst I went to Florence, Mary wrote, but I did not see her letter. Well, good bye. Next Monday I shall write to you from Florence. Love to all.

Most affectionately your friend,

P. B. S.

XXV

To John Gisborne.

Florence, 16th November, 1819.

My dear Sir,

I envy you the first reading of Theocritus. Were not the Greeks a glorious people? What is there, as Job says of the Leviathan, like unto them? If the army of Nicias had not been defeated under the walls of Syracuse; if the Athenians had, acquiring Sicily, held the balance between Rome and Carthage, sent garrisons to the Greek colonies in the south of Italy, Rome might have been all that its intellectual condition entitled it to be, a tributary, not the conqueror of Greece; the Macedonian power would never have attained to the dictatorship of the civilised states of the world. Who knows whether, under the steady progress which philosophy and social institutions would have made—for, in the age to which I refer, their progress was most rapid and secure—among a people of the most perfect physical organisation, whether the Christian religion would have arisen, or the barbarians have overwhelmed the wrecks of civilisation which had survived the conquest and tyranny of the Romans? What, then, should we have been? As it is, all of us who are worth anything, spend our manhood in unlearning the follies, or expiating the mistakes of our youth. We are stuffed full of prejudices; and our natural passions are so managed, that if we restrain them we grow intolerant and precise, because we restrain them not according to reason, but according to error; and if we do not restrain them we do all sorts of mischief to ourselves and others. Our imagination and understanding are alike subjected to rules the most absurd; so much for Theocritus and the Greeks. * * *

Most faithfully your obliged,

P. B. S.

XXVI

To LEIGH HUNT.

Florence, November, 1819.

MY DEAR FRIEND,

Two letters, both bearing date Oct. 20, arrive on the same day:—one is always glad of twins.

We hear of a box arrived at Genoa with books and clothes; it must be yours. Meanwhile the babe is wrapt in flannel petticoats, and we get on with him as we can. He is small, healthy and pretty. Mary is recovering rapidly. Marianne, I hope, is quite well.

You do not tell me whether you have received my lines on the Manchester affair. They are of the exoteric species, and are meant, not for the "Indicator," but the "Examiner." I would send for the former, if you like, some letters on such subjects of art as suggest themselves in Italy. Perhaps I will, at a venture, send you a specimen of what I mean next post. I enclose you in this a piece for the "Examiner," or let it share the fate, whatever that fate may be, of the "Mask of Anarchy."

I am sorry to hear that you have employed

yourself in translating the "Aminta," though I doubt not it will be a just and beautiful translation. You ought to write Amintas. You ought to exercise your fancy in the perpetual creation of new forms of gentleness and beauty.

* * * * * *

With respect to translation, even I will not be seduced by it; although the Greek plays, and some of the ideal dramas of Calderon, with which I have lately, and with inexpressible wonder and delight, become acquainted, are perpetually tempting me to throw over their perfect and glowing forms the grey veil of my own words. And you know me too well to suspect that I refrain from a belief that what I could substitute for them would deserve the regret which yours would, if suppressed. I have confidence in my moral sense alone; but that is a kind of originality. I have only translated the "Cyclops" of Euripides when I could absolutely do nothing else, and the "Symposium" of Plato, which is the delight and astonishment of all who read it:—I mean the original, or so much of the original as is seen in my translation, not the translation itself.

* * * * * *

I think I have had an accession of strength since my residence in Italy, though the disease itself in the side, whatever it may be, is not subdued. Some day we shall all return from Italy. I fear that in England things will be carried violently by the rulers, and they will not have learned to yield in time to the spirit of the age. The great thing to do is to hold the balance between popular impatience and tyrannical obstinacy; to inculcate with fervour both the right of resistance and the duty of forbearance. You know my principles incite me to take all the good I can get in politics, for ever aspiring to something more. I am one of those whom nothing will fully satisfy, but who are ready to be partially satisfied in all that is practicable. We shall see.

Give Bessy a thousand thanks from me for writing out in that pretty neat hand your kind and powerful defence. Ask what she would like best from Italian land. We mean to bring you all something; and Mary and I have been wondering what it shall be. Do you, each of you, choose.

* * * * * *

Adieu, my dear Friend,
Yours affectionately ever,
P. B. S.

XXVII

To EDMUND OLLIER.

Pisa, 14th May, 1820.

DEAR SIR,

I reply to your letter by return of post, to confirm what I said in a former letter respecting a new edition of the "Cenci," which ought, by all means, to be instantly urged forward.

I see by your account that I have been greatly mistaken in my calculations of the profit of my writings. As to the trifle due to me, it may as well remain in your hands.

As to the printing of the "Prometheus," be it as you will. But, in this case, I shall repose on trust in your care respecting the correction of the press; especially in the lyrical parts, where a minute error would be of much consequence. Mr. Gisborne will revise it; he heard it recited, and will therefore more readily seize any error.

If I had even intended to publish "Julian and Maddalo" with my name, yet I would not print it with "Prometheus." It would not harmonize. It is an attempt in a different style, in which I am not yet sure of myself, a *sermo pedestris* way of treating human nature, quite opposed to the idealisms of that drama. If you print "Julian and Maddalo," I wish it to be printed in some unostentatious form, accompanied with the fragment of "Athanase," and exactly in the manner in which I sent it; and I particularly desire that my name may not be annexed to the first edition of it, in any case.

If "Peter Bell" be printed—you can best judge if it will sell or no, and there would be no other reason for printing such a trifle—attend, I pray you, particularly to completely concealing the author; and for Emma read Betty, as the name of Peter's sister. Emma, I recollect, is the real name of a sister of a great poet who might be mistaken for Peter. I ought to say that I send you poems in a few posts, to print at the end of "Prometheus," better fitted for that purpose than any in your possession.

Keats, I hope, is going to show himself a great poet; like the sun to burst through the clouds, which, though dyed in the finest colours of the air, obscured his rising. The Gisbornes will bring me from you copies of whatever may be published when they leave England.

     Dear Sir,
      Yours faithfully,
       P. B. SHELLEY.

XXVIII

To THOMAS MEDWIN.

Pisa, 20th July, 1820.

MY DEAR MEDWIN,

I wrote to you a day or two ago at Geneva. I have since received your letter from the mountains. How much I envy you, or rather how much I sympathize in the delights of your wandering! I have a passion for such expeditions, although partly the capriciousness of my health, and partly the want of the incitement of a companion, keep me at home. I see the mountains, the sky, and the trees from my windows, and recollect, as an old man does the mistress of his youth, the raptures of a more familiar intercourse, but without his regrets, for their forms are yet living in my mind. I hope you will not pass Tuscany, leaving your promised visit unpaid. I leave it to you to make the project of taking up your abode with such an animal of the other world as I am, agreeable to your friend; but Mrs. Shelley unites with me in assuring both yourself and him that, whatever else may be found deficient, a sincere welcome is at least in waiting for you.

I am delighted with your approbation of my
"Cenci," and am encouraged to wish to present
you with "Prometheus Unbound," a drama also,
but a composition of a totally different character.
I do not know if it be wise to affect variety in
compositions, or whether the attempt to excel in
many ways does not debar from excellence in one
particular kind. "Prometheus Unbound" is in the
merest spirit of ideal poetry, and not, as the name
would indicate, a mere imitation of the Greek
drama; nor, indeed, if I have been successful, is it
an imitation of anything. But you will judge. I
hear it is just printed, and I probably shall receive
copies from England before I see you. Your
objection to the "Cenci," as to the introduction of
the name of God, is good, inasmuch as the play
is addressed to a Protestant people; but *we*
Catholics speak eternally and familiarly of the first
person of the Trinity, and, amongst *us*, religion
is more interwoven with, and is less extraneous
to, the system of ordinary life. As to Cenci's
curse, I know not whether I can defend it or no.
I wish I may be able; and, as it often happens
respecting the worst part of an author's work, it
is a particular favourite with me. I prided myself,
as since your approbation I hope that I had just
cause to do, upon the two concluding lines of

the play. I confess I cannot approve of the squeamishness which excludes the exhibition of such subjects from the scene, a squeamishness, the produce, as I firmly believe, of a lower tone of the public mind, and foreign to the majestic and confident wisdom of the golden age of our country. What think you of my boldness? I mean to write a play, in the spirit of human nature, without prejudice or passion, entitled " Charles the First." So vanity intoxicates people; but let those few who praise my verses, and in whose approbation I take so much delight, answer for the sin.

I wonder what in the world the Queen has done.... What silly stuff is this to employ a great nation about. I wish the King and the Queen, like Punch and his wife, would fight out their disputes in person....

Your affectionate friend,
P. B. S.

XXIX

To JOHN KEATS.

Pisa, 27th July, 1820.

MY DEAR KEATS,

I hear with great pain the dangerous accident you have undergone, and Mr. Gisborne, who gives me the account of it, adds that you continue to wear a consumptive appearance. This consumption is a disease particularly fond of people who write such good verses as you have done, and with the assistance of an English winter it can often indulge its selection. I do not think that young and amiable poets are bound to gratify its taste; they have entered into no bond with the Muses to that effect. But seriously, for I am joking on what I am very anxious about, I think you would do well to pass the winter in Italy and avoid so tremendous an accident, and if you think it as necessary as I do, so long as you continue to find Pisa or its neighbourhood agreeable to you, Mrs. Shelley unites with myself in urging the request that you would take up your residence with us. You might come by sea to Leghorn (France is not worth seeing, and the sea is particularly good for weak lungs), which is within a few miles of us. You ought, at all events, to see Italy, and your health, which I suggest as a motive, may be an excuse to you. I spare declamation about the statues, and paintings, and ruins, and what is a greater piece of forbearance, about the mountains and streams, the fields, the colours of the sky, and the sky itself.

I have lately read your "Endymion" again, and even with a new sense of the treasure of poetry it contains, though treasures poured forth with indistinct profusion. This people in general will not endure, and that is the cause of the comparatively few copies which have been sold. I feel persuaded that you are capable of the greatest things, so you but will. I always tell Ollier to send you copies of my books. "Prometheus Unbound" I imagine you will receive nearly at the same time with this letter. The "Cenci" I hope you have already received, it was studiously composed in a different style.

"Below the good how far! but far above the great!"

In poetry I have sought to avoid system and mannerism. I wish those who excel me in genius would pursue the same plan.

Whether you remain in England, or journey

to Italy, believe that you carry with you my anxious wishes for your health, happiness, and success wherever you are, or whatever you undertake, and that I am,

Yours sincerely,
P. B. Shelley.

XXX

To THE EDITOR OF THE "QUARTERLY REVIEW."

SIR,

Should you cast your eye on the signature of this letter before you read the contents, you might imagine that they related to a slanderous paper which appeared in your Review some time since. I never notice anonymous attacks. The wretch who wrote it has doubtless the additional reward of a consciousness of his motives, besides the thirty guineas a sheet or whatever it is that you pay him. Of course you cannot be answerable for all the writings which you edit, and I certainly bear you no ill-will for having edited the abuse to which I allude—indeed, I was too much amused by being compared to Pharaoh, not readily to forgive editor, printer, publisher, stitcher, or any one, except the despicable writer, connected with something so exquisitely entertaining. Seriously speaking, I am not in the habit of permitting myself to be disturbed by what is said or written of me, though, I dare say, I may be condemned sometimes justly enough. But I feel in respect to the writer in question, that "I am there sitting, where he durst not soar."

The case is different with the unfortunate subject of this letter, the author of "Endymion," to whose feelings and situation I entreat you to allow me to call your attention. I write considerably in the dark; but if it is Mr. Gifford that I am addressing, I am persuaded that in an appeal to his humanity and justice, he will acknowledge the "fas ab hoste doceri." I am aware that the first duty of a reviewer is towards the public, and I am willing to confess that the "Endymion" is a poem considerably defective, and that, perhaps, it deserved as much censure as the pages of your Review record against it; but, not to mention that there is a certain contemptuousness of phraseology from which it is difficult for a critic to abstain, in the review of "Endymion," I do not think that the writer has given it its due praise. Surely the poem, with all its faults, is a very remarkable production for a man of Keats's age, and the promise of ultimate excellence is such as has rarely been afforded even by such as have afterwards attained high literary eminence. Look at Book II. line 833, &c., and then Book III. line 113 to 120; read down that page, and then again from line 193. I could cite many other passages, to convince you that it deserved milder usage. Why it should have been reviewed at all, excepting for the purpose of bringing its excellencies into notice, I cannot conceive, for it was very little read, and there was no danger that it should become a model to the age of that false taste, with which I confess that it is replenished.

Poor Keats was thrown into a dreadful state of mind by this review, which, I am persuaded, was not written with any intention of producing the effect, to which it has, at least, greatly contributed, of embittering his existence, and inducing a disease from which there are now but faint hopes of his recovery. The first effects are described to me to have resembled insanity, and it was by assiduous watching that he was restrained from effecting purposes of suicide. The agony of his sufferings at length produced the rupture of a blood-vessel in the lungs, and the usual process of consumption appears to have begun. He is coming to pay me a visit in Italy; but I fear that unless his mind can be kept tranquil, little is to be hoped from the mere influence of climate.

But let me not extort anything from your pity. I have just seen a second volume, published by him evidently in careless despair. I have desired my bookseller to send you a copy, and allow me to solicit your especial attention to the fragment of a poem entitled "Hyperion," the composition of which was checked by the review in question. The great proportion of this piece is surely in the very highest style of poetry. I speak impartially, for the canons of taste to which Keats has conformed in his other compositions are the very reverse of my own. I leave you to judge for yourself: it would be an insult to you to suppose that from motives however honourable you would lend yourself to a deception of the public.

* * * * * *

XXXI

To JOHN GISBORNE.

Pisa, Oggi, November 1820.

MY DEAR SIR,

I send you the "Phaedon" and Tacitus. I congratulate you on your conquest of the "Iliad." You must have been astonished at the perpetually increasing magnificence of the last seven books. Homer there truly begins to be himself. The battle of the Scamander, the funeral of Patroclus, and the high and solemn close of the whole bloody tale in tenderness and inexpiable sorrow, are wrought in a manner incomparable with anything of the same kind. The "Odyssey" is sweet, but there is nothing like this.

I am bathing myself in the light and odour of the flowery and starry Autos. I have read them all more than once. Henry will tell you how much I am in love with Pacchiani. I suffer from my disease considerably. Henry will also tell you how much, and how whimsically, he alarmed me last night.

My kindest remembrances to Mrs. Gisborne, and best wishes for your health and happiness.

Faithfully yours, P. B. S.

I have a new Calderon coming from Paris.

XXXII

To Thomas Love Peacock.

Pisa, 15th February, 1821.

My dear Peacock,

The last letter I received from you, nearly four months from the date thereof, reached me by the boxes which the Gisbornes sent by sea. I am happy to learn that you continue in good external and internal preservation. I received at the same time your printed denunciations against general, and your written ones against particular, poetry; and I agree with you as decidedly in the latter as I differ in the former. The man whose critical gall is not stirred up by such ottava rimas as ——'s may safely be conjectured to possess no gall at all. The world is pale with the sickness of such stuff. At the same time, your anathemas against poetry itself excited me to a sacred rage, or *cacoethes scribendi* of vindicating the insulted Muses. I had the greatest possible desire to break a lance with you, within the lists of a magazine, in honour of my mistress Urania; but God willed that I should be too lazy, and wrested the victory from your hope: since first having unhorsed poetry, and the universal sense of the wisest in all ages, an easy conquest would have remained to you in me, the knight of the shield of shadow and the lance of gossamere. Besides, I was at that moment reading Plato's " Ion," which I recommend you to reconsider. Perhaps in the comparison of Platonic and Malthusian doctrines, the "mavis errare" of Cicero is a justifiable argument; but I have a whole quiver of arguments on such a subject.

Have you seen Godwin's answer to the apostle of the rich? And what do you think of it? It has not yet reached me, nor has your box, of which I am in daily expectation.

We are now in the crisis and point of expectation in Italy. The Neapolitan and Austrian armies are rapidly approaching each other, and every day the news of a battle may be expected. The former have advanced into the ecclesiastical states, and taken hostages from Rome to assure themselves of the neutrality of that power, and appear determined to try their strength in open battle. I need not tell you how little chance there is that the new and undisciplined levies of Naples should stand against a superior force of veteran troops. But the birth of liberty in nations abounds in examples of a reversal of the ordinary laws of calculation: the defeat of the Austrians would be the signal of insurrection throughout all Italy.

I am devising literary plans of some magnitude. But nothing is more difficult and unwelcome than to write without a confidence of finding readers; and if my play of the " Cenci " found none or few, I despair of ever producing anything that shall merit them.

Among your anathemas of the modern attempts in poetry, do you include Keats's " Hyperion " ? I think it very fine. His other poems are worth little; but if the " Hyperion " be not grand poetry, none has been produced by our contemporaries.

I suppose you are writing nothing but Indian laws, &c. I have but a faint idea of your occupation; but I suppose it has much to do with pen and ink.

Mary desires to be kindly remembered to you; and I remain, my dear Peacock,

Yours very faithfully,
P. B. SHELLEY.

XXXIII

To EDMUND OLLIER.

Pisa, 16th Feb., 1821.

DEAR SIR,

I send you three poems, " Ode to Naples," a sonnet, and a longer piece, entitled " Epipsychidion." The two former are my own; and you will be so obliging as to take the first opportunity of publishing according to your own discretion.

The longer poem, I desire, should not be considered as my own; indeed, in a certain sense, it is a production of a portion of me already dead; in this sense the advertisement is no fiction. It is to be published simply for the esoteric few; and I make its author a secret, to avoid the malignity of those who turn sweet food into poison; transforming all they touch into the corruption of their own natures. My wish with respect to it is, that it should be printed immediately in the simplest form, and merely one hundred copies : those who are capable of judging and feeling rightly with respect to a composition of so abstruse a nature, certainly do not arrive at that number—among those, at least, who would ever be excited to read an obscure and anonymous production; and it would give me no pleasure that the vulgar should read it. If you have any bookselling reason against publishing so small a number as a hundred, merely distribute copies among those to whom you think the poetry would afford any pleasure, and send me, as soon as you can, a copy by the post. I have written it so as to give very little trouble, I hope, to the printer, or to the person who revises. I should be much obliged to you if you would take this office on yourself.

Is there any expectation of a second edition of the "Revolt of Islam"? I have many corrections to make in it, and one part will be wholly remodelled. I am employed in high and new designs in verse; but they are the labours of years, perhaps.

We expect here every day the news of a battle between the armies of Austria and Naples. The latter have advanced upon Rome; and the first affair will probably take place in the ecclesiastical states. You may imagine the expectation of all here.

Pray send me news of my intellectual children. For "Prometheus," I expect and desire no great sale. The "Cenci" ought to have been popular.

I remain, dear Sir,
Your very obedient servant,
PERCY B. SHELLEY.

XXXIV

To THOMAS LOVE PEACOCK.

Pisa, 21st March, 1821.

MY DEAR PEACOCK,

I despatch by this post the first part of an essay intended to consist of three parts, which I design for an antidote to your "Four Ages of Poetry." You will see that I have taken a more general view of what is poetry than you have, and will perhaps agree with several of my positions without considering your own touched. But read and judge; and do not let us imitate the great founders of the picturesque, Price and Payne Knight, who, like two ill-trained beagles, began snarling at each other when they could not catch the hare.

I hear the welcome news of a box from England announced by Mr. Gisborne. How much new poetry does it contain? The Bavii and Maevii of the day are very fertile; and I wish those who honour me with boxes would read and inwardly digest your "Four Ages of Poetry;" for I had much rather, for my own private reading, receive political, geological, and moral treatises than this stuff in terza, ottava, and tremillesima rima whose earthly baseness has attracted the lightning of your undiscriminating censure upon the temple of immortal song. . . .

Do you see much of Hogg now? And the Boinvilles and Coulson? Hunt I suppose not. And are you occupied as much as ever? We are surrounded here in Pisa by revolutionary volcanoes, which, as yet, give more light than heat; the lava has reached Tuscany. But the news in the papers will tell you far more than it is prudent for me to say; and for this once I will observe your rule of political silence. The Austrians wish that the Neapolitans and Piedmontese would do the same.

We have seen a few more people than usual this winter, and have made a very interesting acquaintance with a Greek prince, perfectly acquainted with ancient literature, and full of enthusiasm for the liberties and improvement of his country. Mary has been a Greek student for several months, and is reading "Antigone" with our turbaned friend, who, in return, is taught English. Claire has passed the Carnival at Florence, and has been preternaturally gay. I have had a severe ophthalmia, and have read or written little this winter; and have made acquaintance in an obscure convent with the only Italian for whom I ever felt any interest.

I want you to do something for me : that is, to get me two pounds' worth of Tassie's gems, in Leicester Square, the prettiest, according to your taste ; among them the head of Alexander ; and to get me two seals engraved and set, one smaller, and the other handsomer ; the device a dove with outspread wings, and this motto round it :

μαντις ειμ' εσθλων αγωνων.

Mary desires her best regards ; and I remain, my dear Peacock, ever most sincerely yours,

P. B. S.

XXXV

To Mr. and Mrs. Gisborne.

Bagni, 19th July, 1821.

My dearest Friends,

I am fully repaid for the painful emotions from which such verses of my poem sprung, by your sympathy and approbation, which is all the reward I expect, as much as I desire. It is not for me to judge whether, in the high praise your feelings assign me, you are right or wrong. The poet and the man are two different natures; though they exist together, they may be unconscious of each other, and incapable of deciding on each other's powers and efforts by any reflex act. The decision of the cause, whether or no I am a poet, is removed from the present time to the hour when our posterity shall assemble; but the court is a very severe one, and I fear that the verdict will be, "guilty, death!"

I shall be with you on the first summons. I hope that the time you have reserved for us, "this bank and shoal of time," is not so short as you once talked of.

In haste, most affectionately yours,

P. B. S.

XXXVI

To Mrs. Shelley.

Ravenna, 7th August, 1821.

My dearest Mary,

I arrived last night at ten o'clock, and sat up talking with Lord Byron until five this morning. I then went to sleep, and now awake at eleven, and having despatched my breakfast as quick as possible, mean to devote the interval till twelve, when the post departs, to you.

Lord Byron is very well, and was delighted to see me. He has in fact completely recovered his health, and lives a life totally the reverse of that which he led at Venice. He has a permanent sort of liaison with Contessa Guiccioli, who is now at Florence, and seems from her letters to be a very amiable woman. She is waiting there until something suitable shall be decided as to their emigration to Switzerland or stay in Italy; which is yet undetermined on either side. She was compelled to escape from the Papal territory in great haste, as measures had already been taken to place her in a convent, where she would have been unrelentingly confined for life. The oppression of the marriage contract, as existing in the laws and opinions of Italy, though less frequently exercised, is far severer than that of England. I tremble to think of what poor Emilia is destined to.

Lord Byron had almost destroyed himself in Venice: his state of debility was such that he was unable to digest any food, he was consumed by hectic fever, and would speedily have perished, but for this attachment, which has reclaimed him from the excesses into which he threw himself from carelessness and pride, rather than taste. Poor fellow! He is now quite well, and immersed in politics and literature. He has given me a number of the most interesting details on the former subject, but we will not speak of them in a letter. Fletcher is here; and as if, like a shadow, he waxed and waned with the substance of his master, Fletcher also has recovered his good looks, and from amidst the unseasonable grey hairs, a fresh harvest of flaxen locks has put forth.

We talked a great deal of poetry and such matters last night; and as usual differed, and I think more than ever. He affects to patronize a system of criticism fit for the production of mediocrity, and although all his fine poems and passages have been produced in defiance of this system, yet I recognise the pernicious effects of it in the "Doge of Venice;" and it will cramp and limit his future efforts however great they may be, unless he gets rid of it. I have read only parts of it, or rather he himself read them to me, and gave me the plan of the whole.

* * * * * *

XXXVII

To Mrs. Shelley.

Friday, 10th August, 1821.

We ride out in the evening, through the pine forests which divide this city from the sea. Our way of life is this, and I have accommodated myself to it without much difficulty :—Lord Byron gets up at two, breakfasts; we talk, read, &c., until six; then we ride, and dine at eight; and after dinner sit talking till four or five in the morning. I get up at twelve, and am now devoting the interval between my rising and his, to you.

Lord Byron is greatly improved in every respect —in genius, in temper, in moral views, in health, in happiness. The connexion with La Guiccioli has been an inestimable benefit to him. He lives with considerable splendour, but within his income, which is now about 4000*l.* a year, 1000*l.* of which he devotes to purposes of charity. He has had mischievous passions, but these he seems to have subdued, and he is becoming, what he should be, a virtuous man. The interest which he took in the politics of Italy, and the actions he performed in consequence of it, are subjects not fit to be written, but are such as will delight and surprise you. He is not yet decided to go to Switzerland, a place, indeed, little fitted for him : the gossip and the cabals of those anglicized coteries would torment him, as they did before, and might exasperate him to a relapse of libertinism, which he says he plunged into not from taste, but despair. La Guiccioli and her brother, who is Lord Byron's friend and confidant, and acquiesces perfectly in her connection with him, wish to go to Switzerland; as Lord Byron says, merely from the novelty of the pleasure of travelling. Lord Byron prefers Tuscany or Lucca, and is trying to persuade them to adopt his views. He has made me write a long letter to her to engage her to remain, an odd thing enough for an utter stranger to write on subjects of the utmost delicacy to his friend's mistress. But it seems destined that I am always to have some active part in everybody's affairs whom I approach. I have set down in lame Italian the strongest reasons I can think of against the Swiss emigration ; to tell you truth, I should be very glad to accept, as my fee, his establishment in Tuscany. Ravenna is a miserable place ; the people are barbarous and wild, and their language the most infernal patois that you can imagine. He would be, in every respect, better among the Tuscans. . . .

He has read to me one of the unpublished cantos of "Don Juan," which is astonishingly fine. It sets him not only above, but far above, all the poets of the day, every word has the stamp of immortality. I despair of rivalling Lord Byron, as well I may, and there is no other with whom it is worth contending. This canto is in the style, but totally, and sustained with incredible ease and power, like the end of the second canto. There is not a word which the most rigid assertor of the dignity of human nature could desire to be cancelled. It fulfils, in a certain degree, what I have long preached of producing, something wholly new and relative to the age, and yet surpassingly beautiful. It may be vanity, but I think I see the trace of my earnest exhortations to him to create something wholly new. He has finished his Life up to the present time, and given it to Moore, with liberty for Moore to sell it at the best price he can get, with condition that the bookseller shall publish it after his death. Moore has sold it to Murray for two thousand pounds. I wish I had been in time to have interceded for a part of it for poor Hunt. I have spoken to him of Hunt, but not with a direct view of demanding a contribution; and, though I am sure that if asked it would not be refused, yet there is something in me that makes it impossible. Lord Byron and I are excellent friends, and were I reduced to poverty, or were I a writer who had no claims to an higher station than I possess, or did I possess an higher than I deserve, we should appear in all things as such, and I would freely ask him any favour. Such is not now the case. The daemon of mistrust and pride lurks between two persons in our situation, poisoning the freedom of our intercourse. This is a tax and a heavy one, which we must pay for being human. I think the fault is not on my side, nor is it likely, I being the weaker. I hope that in the next world these things will be better managed. What is passing in the heart of another rarely escapes the observation of one who is a strict anatomist of his own.

Write to me at Florence, where I shall remain a day at least, and send me letters, or news of letters. How is my little darling? And how are you, and how do you get on with your book? Be severe in your corrections, and expect severity from me, your sincere admirer. I flatter myself you have composed something unequalled in its kind, and that, not content with the honours of your birth and your hereditary aristocracy, you will add still higher renown to your name.

Expect me at the end of my appointed time. I do not think I shall be detained. Is Claire with you, or is she coming? Have you heard anything of my poor Emilia, from whom I got a letter the day of my departure, saying that her marriage was deferred for a very short time, on account of the illness of her *sposo*. How are the Williamses, and Williams especially? Give my kindest love to them.

Lord Byron has here splendid apartments in the palace of his mistress's husband, who is one of the richest men in Italy. She is divorced, with an allowance of 1200 crowns a year, a miserable pittance from a man who has 120,000 a year. Here are two monkeys, five cats, eight dogs, and ten horses, all of whom, except the horses, walk about the house like the masters of it. Tita the Venetian is here, and operates as my valet; a fine fellow, with a prodigious black beard, and who has stabbed two or three people, and is the most good-natured looking fellow I ever saw.

We have good rumours of the Greeks here, and a Russian war. I hardly wish the Russians to take any part in it. My maxim is with Aeschylus:—

το δυσσεβες—
μετ ι μεν πλειονα τικτει,
σφετερα δ' εικοτα γεννα.

There is a Greek exercise for you. How should slaves produce anything but tyranny, even as the seed produces the plant?

    Adieu, dear Mary,
      Yours affectionately,
        S.

XXXVIII

To Thomas Love Peacock.

Ravenna, [*10th August, 1821.*]

My dear Peacock,

I received your last letter just as I was setting off from the Bagni on a visit to Lord Byron at this place. Many thanks for all your kind attention to my accursed affairs. . . .

I have sent you by the Gisbornes a copy of the elegy on Keats. The subject, I know, will not please you; but the composition of the poetry, and the taste in which it is written I do not think bad. You and the enlightened public will judge. Lord Byron is in excellent cue both of health and spirits. He has got rid of all those melancholy and degrading habits which he indulged at Venice. He lives with one woman, a lady of rank here, to whom he is attached, and who is attached to him, and is in every respect an altered man. He has written three more cantos of "Don Juan." I have yet only heard the fifth, and I think that every word of it is pregnant with immortality. I have not seen his late plays, except "Marino Faliero," which is very well, but not so transcendently fine as the "Don Juan."

Lord Byron gets up at two. I get up—quite contrary to my usual custom, but one must sleep or die, like Southey's sea-snake in Kehama—at twelve. After breakfast, we sit talking till six. From six till eight we gallop through the pine forests which divide Ravenna from the sea; we then come home and dine, and sit up gossiping till six in the morning. I don't suppose this will kill me in a week or fortnight, but I shall not try it longer. Lord B.'s establishment consists, besides servants, of ten horses, eight enormous dogs, five cats, an eagle, a crow, and a falcon; and all these, except the horses, walk about the house, which every now and then resounds with their unarbitrated quarrels, as if they were the masters of it. Lord B. thinks you wrote a pamphlet signed " John Bull;" he says he knew it by the style resembling "Melincourt," of which he is a great admirer. I read it, and assured him that it could not possibly be yours. I write nothing, and probably shall write no more. It offends me to see my name classed among those who have no name. If I cannot be something better, I had rather be nothing. . . . and the accursed cause to the downfall of which I dedicated what powers I may have had, flourishes like a cedar and covers England with its boughs. My motive was never the infirm desire of fame; and if I should continue an author, I feel that I should desire it. This cup is justly given to one only of an age; indeed, participation would make it worthless; and unfortunate they who seek it and find it not.

I congratulate you, I hope I ought to do so, on your expected stranger. He is introduced into a rough world. My regards to Hogg, and Coulson if you see him.

Ever most faithfully yours,
P. B. S.

After I have sealed my letter, I find that my enumeration of the animals in this Circaean palace was defective, and that in a material point. I have just met on the grand staircase five peacocks, two guinea-hens, and an Egyptian crane. I wonder who all these animals were, before they were changed into these shapes.

XXXIX

To Mrs. Shelley.

Ravenna, 15th Aug., 1821.

* * * * * *

I went the other day to see Allegra at her convent, and stayed with her about three hours. She is grown tall and slight for her age, and her face is somewhat altered. The traits have become more delicate, and she is much paler, probably from the effect of improper food. She yet retains the beauty of her deep blue eyes and of her mouth, but she has a contemplative seriousness which, mixed with her excessive vivacity, which has not yet deserted her, has a very peculiar effect in a child. She is under very strict discipline, as may be observed from the immediate obedience she accords to the will of her attendants. This seems contrary to her nature, but I do not think it has been obtained at the expense of much severity. Her hair, scarcely darker than it was, is beautifully profuse, and hangs in large curls on her neck. She was prettily dressed in white muslin, and an apron of black silk, with trousers. Her light and airy figure and her graceful motions were a striking contrast to the other children there.

She seemed a thing of a finer and a higher order. At first she was very shy, but after a little caressing, and especially after I had given her a gold chain which I had bought at Ravenna for her, she grew more familiar, and led me all over the garden, and all over the convent, running and skipping so fast that I could hardly keep up with her. She showed me her little bed, and the chair where she sat at dinner, and the carozzina in which she and her favourite companions drew each other along a walk in the garden. I had brought her a basket of sweetmeats, and before eating any of them she gave her companions and each of the nuns a portion. This is not much like the old Allegra. I asked her what I should say from her to her mamma, and she said:—

"Che mi manda un bacio e un bel vestituro."

"E come vuoi il vestituro sia fatto?"

"Tutto di seta e d' oro," was her reply.

Her predominant foible seems the love of distinction and vanity, and this is a plant which produces good or evil, according to the gardener's skill. I then asked her what I should say to papa? "Che venga farmi un visitino e che porta seco la *mammina*." Before I went away she made me run all over the convent, like a mad thing. The nuns, who were half in bed, were ordered to hide themselves, and on returning Allegra began ringing the bell which calls the nuns to assemble. The tocsin of the convent sounded, and it required all the efforts of the Prioress to prevent the spouses of God from rendering themselves, dressed or undressed, to the accustomed signal. Nobody scolded her for these *scappature*, so I suppose she is well treated, so far as temper is concerned. Her intellect is not much cultivated. She knows certain *orazioni* by heart, and talks and dreams of Paradiso and all sorts of things, and has a prodigious list of saints, and is always talking of the Bambino. This will do her no harm, but the idea of bringing up so sweet a creature in the midst of such trash till sixteen !

XL

To Leigh Hunt.

Pisa, 26th August, 1821.

MY DEAREST FRIEND,

Since I last wrote to you, I have been on a visit to Lord Byron at Ravenna. The result of this visit was a determination on his part to come and live at Pisa; and I have taken the finest palace on the Lung' Arno for him. But the material part of my visit consists in a message which he desires me to give you, and which I think ought to add to your determination, for such a one I hope you have formed, of restoring your shattered health and spirits by a migration to these "regions mild of calm and serene air."

He proposes that you should come and go shares with him and me in a periodical work, to be conducted here; in which each of the contracting parties should publish all their original compositions, and share the profits. He proposed it to Moore, but for some reason it was never brought to bear. There can be no doubt that the profits of any scheme in which you and Lord Byron engage, must, from various, yet co-operating reasons, be very great. As for myself, I am, for the present, only a sort of link between you and him, until you can know each other and effectuate the arrangement; since, to intrust you with a secret which, for your sake, I withhold from Lord Byron, nothing would induce me to share in the profits, and still less in the borrowed splendour of such a partnership. You and he, in different manners, would be equal, and would bring, in a different manner, but in the same proportion, equal stocks of reputation and success. Do not let my frankness with you, nor my belief that you deserve it more than Lord Byron, have the effect of deterring you from assuming a station in modern literature, which the universal voice of my contemporaries forbids me either to stoop or to aspire to. I am, and I desire to be, nothing.

I did not ask Lord Byron to assist me in sending a remittance for your journey; because there are men, however excellent, from whom we would never receive an obligation, in the worldly sense of the word; and I am as jealous for my friend as for myself. I, as you know, have it not: but I suppose that at last I shall make up an impudent face, and ask Horace Smith to add to the many obligations he has conferred on me. I know I need only ask.

I think I have never told you how very much

I like your "Amyntas;" it almost reconciles me to translations. In another sense, I still demur. You might have written another such poem as the "Nymphs," with no great access of effort. I am full of thoughts and plans, and should do something if the feeble and irritable frame which incloses it was willing to obey the spirit. I fancy that then I should do great things. Before this you will have seen "Adonais." Lord Byron, I suppose from modesty on account of his being mentioned in it, did not say a word of "Adonais," though he was loud in his praise of "Prometheus:" and, what you will not agree with him in, censure of the "Cenci." Certainly, if "Marino Faliero" is a drama, the "Cenci" is not: but that between ourselves. Lord Byron is reformed, as far as gallantry goes, and lives with a beautiful and sentimental Italian lady, who is as much attached to him as may be. I trust greatly to his intercourse with you, for his creed to become as pure as he thinks his conduct is. He has many generous and exalted qualities, but the canker of aristocracy wants to be cut out.

* * * * * *

XLI

To Edmund Ollier.

Pisa, 25th September, 1821.

Dear Sir,

It will give me great pleasure if I can arrange the affair of Mrs. Shelley's novel with you to her and your satisfaction. She has a specific purpose in the sum which she instructed me to require; and, although this purpose could not be answered without ready money, yet I should find means to answer her wishes in that point, if you could make it convenient to pay one-third at Christmas, and give bills for the other two-thirds at twelve and eighteen months. It would give me peculiar satisfaction that you, rather than any other person, should be the publisher of this work; it is the product of no slight labour, and I flatter myself, of no common talent. I doubt not it will give no less credit than it will receive from your names. I trust you know me too well to believe that my judgment deliberately given in testimony of the value of any production is influenced by motives of interest or partiality.

The romance is called "Castruccio, Prince of Lucca," and is founded, not upon the novel of

Macchiavelli under that name, which substitutes a childish fiction for the far more romantic truth of history, but upon the actual story of his life. He was a person who, from an exile and an adventurer, after having served in the wars of England and Flanders in the reign of our Edward the Second, returned to his native city, and, liberating it from its tyrants, became himself its tyrant, and died in the full splendour of his dominion, which he had extended over the half of Tuscany. He was a little Napoleon, and, with a dukedom instead of an empire for his theatre, brought upon the same all the passions and the errors of his antitype. The chief interest of the romance rests upon Euthanasia, his betrothed bride, whose love for him is only equalled by her enthusiasm for the liberty of the republic of Florence, which is in some sort her country, and for that of Italy, to which Castruccio is a devoted enemy, being an ally of the party of the Emperor. This character is a masterpiece; and the key-stone of the drama, which is built up with admirable art, is the conflict between these passions and these principles. Euthanasia, the last survivor of a noble house, is a feudal countess, and her castle is the scene of the exhibition of the knightly manners of the time. The character of Beatrice, the prophetess, can only be done justice to in the very language of the author. I know nothing in Walter Scott's novels which at all approaches to the beauty and the sublimity of this—creation, I may say, for it is perfectly original; and, although founded upon the ideas and manners of the age which is represented, is wholly without a similitude in any fiction I ever read. Beatrice is in love with Castruccio, and dies; for the romance, although interspersed with much lighter matter, is deeply tragic, and the shades darken and gather as the catastrophe approaches. All the manners, customs, opinions of the age are introduced; the superstitions, the heresies, and the religious persecutions are displayed; the minutest circumstance of Italian manners in that age is not omitted; and the whole seems to me to constitute a living and moving picture of an age almost forgotten. The author visited the scenery which she describes in person; and one or two of the inferior characters are drawn from her own observation of the Italians, for the national character shows itself still in certain instances under the same forms as it wore in the time of Dante. The novel consists, as I told you before, of three volumes, each at least equal to one of the " Tales of my Landlord," and they will be very soon ready to be sent. In case you should accept the present offer, I will make one observation which I consider of essential importance. It ought to be printed in half-volumes at a time, and sent to the author for her last corrections by the post. It may be printed on thin paper like that of this letter, and the expense shall fall upon me. Lord Byron has his works sent in this manner; and no person, who has either fame to lose or money to win, ought to publish in any other manner.

By-the-bye, how do I stand with regard to these two great objects of human pursuit? I once sought something nobler and better than either; but I might as well have reached at the moon, and now, finding that I have grasped the air, I should not be sorry to know what substantial sum, especially of the former, is in your hands on my account. The gods have made the reviewers the almoners of this worldly dross, and I think I must write an ode to flatter them to give me some; if I would not that they put me off with a bill on posterity, which when my ghost shall present, the answer will be "No effects."

"Charles the First" is conceived, but not born. Unless I am sure of making something good the play will not be written. Pride, that ruined

Satan, will kill "Charles the First," for his midwife would only be less than him whom thunder has made greater. I am full of great plans; and, if I should tell you them, I should add to the list of these riddles.

I have not seen Mr. Procter's "Mirandola." Send it to me in the box, and pray send me the box immediately. It is of the utmost consequence; and, as you are so obliging as to say you will not neglect my commissions, pray send this without delay. I hope it is sent, indeed, and that you have recollected to send me several copies of "Prometheus," the "Revolt of Islam," and the "Cenci," &c., as I requested you. Is there any chance of a second edition of the "Revolt of Islam"? I could materially improve that poem on revision. The "Adonais," in spite of its mysticism, is the least imperfect of my compositions, and, as the image of my regret and honour for poor Keats, I wish it to be so. I shall write to you, probably, by next post on the subject of that poem, and should have sent the promised criticism for the second edition had I not mislaid, and in vain sought for, the volume that contains "Hyperion." Pray give me notice against what time you want the second part of my "Defence of Poetry." I give you this

"Defence," and you may do what you will with it.

Pray give me an immediate answer about the novel.

> I am, my dear Sir,
> Your very obliged servant,
> PERCY B. SHELLEY.

I ought to tell you that the novel has not the smallest tincture of any peculiar theories in politics or religion.

XLII

To JOHN GISBORNE.

Pisa, 22nd October, 1821.

MY DEAR GISBORNE,

At length the post brings a welcome letter from you, and I am pleased to be assured of your health and safe arrival. I expect with interest and anxiety the intelligence of your progress in England, and how far the advantages there compensate the loss of Italy. I hear from Hunt that he is determined on emigration, and if I thought the letter would arrive in time, should beg you to suggest some advice to him. But you ought to be incapable of forgiving me the fact of depriving England of what it must lose when Hunt departs.

Did I tell you that Lord Byron comes to settle at Pisa, and that he has a plan of writing a periodical work in conjunction with Hunt? His house, Madame Felichi's, is already taken and fitted up for him, and he has been expected every day these six weeks. La Guiccioli, who awaits him impatiently, is a very pretty, sentimental, innocent Italian, who has sacrificed an immense fortune for the sake of Lord Byron, and who, if

I know anything of my friend, will hereafter have plenty of leisure and opportunity to repent her rashness. Lord Byron is, however, quite cured of his gross habits, as far as habits; the perverse ideas on which they were formed are not yet eradicated.

We have furnished a house at Pisa, and mean to make it our head-quarters. I shall get all my books out, and entrench myself like a spider in a web. If you can assist Peacock in sending them to Leghorn, you would do me an especial favour; but do not buy me Calderon, "Faust," or Kant, as Horace Smith proposes to send them me from Paris, where I suppose you had not time to procure them. Any other books you or Henry think would accord with my design, Ollier will furnish you with.

I should like very much to hear what is said of my "Adonais," and you would oblige me by cutting out, or making Ollier cut out, any respectable criticism on it, and sending it me; you know I do not mind a crown or two in postage. The "Epipsychidion" is a mystery; as to real flesh and blood, you know that I do not deal in those articles; you might as well go to a gin-shop for a leg of mutton as expect anything human or earthly from me. I desired Ollier not to circulate this piece except to the συνετοι, and even they, it seems, are inclined to approximate me to the circle of a servant girl and her sweetheart. But I intend to write a symposium of my own to set all this right.

I am just finishing a dramatic poem called "Hellas," upon the contest now raging in Greece, a sort of imitation of the "Persae" of Aeschylus, full of lyrical poetry. I try to be what I might have been, but am not successful. I find that—I dare say I shall quote wrong,—

"Den herrlichsten, den sich der Geist empfängt,
Drängt immer fremd und fremder Stoff sich an."

The "Edinburgh Review" lies. Godwin's answer to Malthus is victorious and decisive; and that it should not be generally acknowledged as such, is full evidence of the influence of successful evil and tyranny. What Godwin is, compared to Plato and Lord Bacon, we well know; but compared with these miserable sciolists, he is a vulture to a worm.

I read the Greek dramatists and Plato for ever. You are right about "Antigone;" how sublime a picture of a woman! and what think you of the choruses, and especially of the lyrical complaints of the godlike victim? and the menaces of Tiresias and their rapid fulfilment? Some of us have, in a prior existence, been in love with an Antigone, and that makes us find no full content in any mortal tie. As to books, I advise you to live near the British Museum and read there. I have read, since I saw you, the "Jungfrau von Orleans" of Schiller, a fine play if the fifth act did not fall off. Some Greeks, escaped from the defeat in Wallachia, have passed through Pisa to re-embark at Leghorn for the Morea; and the Tuscan Government allowed them, during their stay and passage, three lire each per day and their lodging; that is good. Remember me and Mary most kindly to Mrs. Gisborne and Henry, and believe me,

Yours most affectionately,
P. B. S.

XLIII

To Joseph Severn.

Pisa, 29th November, 1821.

Dear Sir,

I send you the elegy on poor Keats, and I wish it were better worth your acceptance. You will see, by the preface, that it was written before I could obtain any particular account of his last moments; all that I still know was communicated to me by a friend who had derived his information from Colonel Finch; I have ventured to express, as I felt, the respect and admiration which your conduct towards him demands.

In spite of his transcendent genius, Keats never was, nor ever will be, a popular poet; and the total neglect and obscurity in which the astonishing remnants of his mind still lie, was hardly to be dissipated by a writer who, however he may differ from Keats in more important qualities, at least resembles him in that accidental one, a want of popularity.

I have little hope, therefore, that the poem I send you will excite any attention, nor do I feel assured that a critical notice of his writings would find a single reader. But for these considerations, it had been my intention to have collected the remnants of his compositions, and to have published them with a life and criticism. Has he left any poems or writings of whatsoever kind, and in whose possession are they? Perhaps you would oblige me by information on this point.

Many thanks for the picture you promise me: I shall consider it among the most sacred relics of the past.

For my part, I little expected, when I last saw Keats at my friend Leigh Hunt's, that I should survive him.

Should you ever pass through Pisa I hope to have the pleasure of seeing you, and of cultivating an acquaintance into something pleasant, begun under such melancholy auspices.

Accept, my dear Sir, the assurance of my sincere esteem, and believe me,
  Your most sincere and faithful servant,
    PERCY B. SHELLEY.

XLIV

To THOMAS LOVE PEACOCK.

Pisa, January [11, 1822].

MY DEAR PEACOCK,

I am still at Pisa, where I have at length fitted up some rooms at the top of a lofty palace that overlooks the city and the surrounding region, and have collected books and plants about me, and established myself for some indefinite time, which, if I read the future, will not be short. I wish you to send my books by the very first opportunity, and I expect in them a great augmentation of comfort. Lord Byron is established here, and we are constant companions. No small relief this, after the dreary solitude of the understanding and the imagination in which we passed the first years of our expatriation, yoked to all sorts of miseries and discomforts.

Of course you have seen his last volume, and if you before thought him a great poet, what is your opinion now that you have read "Cain"? The "Foscari" and "Sardanapalus" I have not seen; but as they are in the style of his later writings, I doubt not they are very fine. We expect Hunt here every day, and remain in great anxiety on account of the heavy gales which he must have encountered at Christmas. Lord Byron has fitted up the lower apartments of his palace for him, and Hunt will be agreeably surprised to find a commodious lodging prepared for him after the fatigues and dangers of his passage. I have been long idle, and, as far as writing goes, despondent; but I am now engaged on "Charles the First," and a devil of a nut it is to crack.

Mary and Clara, who is not with us just at present, are well, and so is our little boy, the image of poor William. We live as usual, tranquilly. I get up, or at least wake, early; read and write till two; dine, go to Lord Byron's, and ride or play at billiards as the weather permits; and sacrifice the evening either to light books or whoever happens to drop in. Our furniture, which is very neat, cost fewer shillings than that at Marlow did pounds sterling; and our windows are full of plants which turn the sunny winter into spring. My health is better, my cares are lighter; and although nothing will cure the consumption of my purse, yet it drags on a sort of life in death, very like its master, and seems, like Fortunatus's, always empty yet never quite exhausted. You will have seen my "Adonais," and perhaps my "Hellas," and I think, whatever you may judge of the subject, the composition of the first poem will not wholly displease you. I wish I had something better to do than furnish this jingling food for the hunger of oblivion, called verse, but I have not; and since you give me no encouragement about India, I cannot hope to have.

How is your little star, and the heaven which contains the milky way in which it glitters?

Adieu. Yours ever most truly,

S.

XLV

To JOHN GISBORNE.

Pisa, January, 1822.

. . . One thing I rejoice to hear, that your health is better. So is mine; but my mind is like an overworked race-horse put into an hackney coach. What think you of Lord Byron now? Space wondered less at the swift and fair creations of God, when he grew weary of vacancy, than I at this spirit of an angel in the mortal paradise of a decaying body. So I think, let the world envy while it admires, as it may.

We have just got the etchings of "Faust;" the painter is worthy of Goethe. The meeting of him and Margaret is wonderful. It makes all the pulses of my head beat, those of my heart have been quiet long ago. The translations, both these and in "Blackwood," are miserable. Ask Coleridge if their stupid misintelligence of the deep wisdom and harmony of the author does not spur him to action. You will have heard of the Hunts, and of all my perplexities about them. The Williamses are well; Mrs. Williams more amiable and beautiful than ever, and a sort of spirit of embodied peace in the midst of our circle of tempests. So much for first impressions!

XLVI

To LEIGH HUNT.

Pisa, Jan. 25, 1822.

MY DEAREST FRIEND,

I send you by return of post 150*l.*, within 30 or 40 of what I had contrived to scrape together. How I am to assemble the constituents of such a sum again I do not at present see; but do not be disheartened, we will all put our shoulders to the wheel. Let me not speak of my own disappointment, which, great as it is at not seeing you here, is all swallowed up in sympathy with your present situation. Our anxiety during the continuance of the succession of tempests which one morning seemed to rain lightnings into Pisa, and amongst others struck the palace adjoining Lord Byron's, and turned the Arno into a raging sea, was, as you may conceive, excessive, and our first relief was your letter from Ramsgate. Between the interval of that and your letter of December 28, we were in daily expectation of your arrival. Yesterday arrived that dated January 6.

Lord Byron had assigned you a portion of his palace, and Mary and I had occupied ourselves in furnishing it. Everything was already provided except bedding, which could have been got in a moment, and which we thought it possible you might bring with you. We had hired a woman cook of the country for you, who is still with us. Lord Byron had kindly insisted upon paying the upholsterer's bill, with that sort of unsuspecting goodness which makes it infinitely difficult to ask him for more. Past circumstances between Lord Byron and me render it impossible that I should accept any supply from him for my own use, or that I should ask it for yours if the contribution could be supposed in any manner to relieve me, or to do what I could otherwise have done. It is true that I cannot, but how is he to be assured of this? One thing strikes me as possible. I am at present writing the drama of "Charles the First," a play which, if completed according to my present idea, will hold a higher rank than the "Cenci" as a work of art. Would no bookseller give me 150*l*. or 200*l*. for the copyright of this play? You know best how my writings sell, whether at all or not: after they failed of making the sort of impression on men that I expected, I have never until now thought it worth while to enquire. The question is now interesting to me, inasmuch as the reputation depending on their sale might induce a bookseller to give me such a sum for this play. Write to Allman, your bookseller, and tell him what I tell you of "Charles the First," and do not delay a post. I have a parcel of little poems also, the "Witch of Atlas," and some translations of Homer's hymns, the copyright of which I must sell. I offered the "Charles the First" to Ollier, and you had better write at the same time to learn his terms. Of course you will not delay a post in this.

The evils of your remaining in England are inconceivably great if you ultimately determine upon Italy; and in the latter case, the best thing you can do is, without waiting for the spring, to set sail with the very first ship you can. Debts, responsibilities, and expenses will enmesh you round about if you delay, and force you back into that circle from which I made a push to draw you. The winter, generally, is not a bad time for sailing, but only that period which you selected, and another when the year approaches to the vernal equinox. You avoided, and if you must still delay, will still avoid, the halcyon days of the Mediterranean. There is no serious danger in a cargo of gunpowder; hundreds of ships navigate these electrical seas with the freight without risk. Marianne would have been benefited, and would still benefit exceedingly, by the elysian temperature of the Mediterranean.

Poor Marianne, how much I feel for her, and with what anxiety I expect your news of her health! Were it not for the cursed necessity of finding money, all considerations would be swallowed up in the thought of her; and I should be delighted to think that she had obtained this interval of repose which now perplexes and annoys me. . . . . .

Pray tell me in answer to this letter, unless you answer it in person, what arrangement you have made about the receipt of a regular income from the profits of the "Examiner." You ought not to leave England without having the assurance of an independence in this particular; as many difficulties have presented themselves to the plan imagined by Lord Byron, which I depend upon you for getting rid of. And if there is time to write before you set off, pray tell me if Ollier has published "Hellas," and what effect was produced by "Adonais." My faculties are shaken to atoms, and torpid. I can write nothing; and if "Adonais" had no success, and excited no interest, what incentive can I have to write? As to reviews, don't give Gifford, or his associate Hazlitt, a stripe the more for my sake. The man must be enviably happy whom reviews can make miserable. I have neither curiosity, interest, pain, nor pleasure in anything, good or evil, they can say of me. I feel only a slight disgust, and a sort of wonder that they presume to write my name. I began once a satire upon satire, which I meant to be very severe; it was full of *small knives*, in the use of which practice would have soon made me very expert.

XLVII

To Horace Smith.

Pisa, 25th January, 1822.

My dear Smith,

I have delayed this fortnight answering your kind letter because I was in treaty for a Calderon, which at last I have succeeded in procuring at a tolerably moderate price. All the other books you mention I should be glad to have, together with whatever others might fall in your way that you might think interesting.

Will you not think my exactions upon your kindness interminable if I ask you to execute another commission for me? It is to buy a good pedal harp without great ornament or any appendage that would unnecessarily increase the expense—but good; nor should I object to its being second-hand, if that were equally compatible with its being despatched immediately. Together with the harp I should wish for five or six napoleons' worth of harp music, at your discretion. I do not know the price of harps at Paris, but I suppose that from 70 to 80 guineas would cover it, and I trust to your accustomed kindness, as I want it for a present, to make the immediate advance, as if I were to delay, the grace of my compliment would be lost. Do not take much trouble about it, but simply take what you find, if you are so exceedingly kind as to oblige me.

It had better be sent by Marseilles, through some merchant or in any other manner you think best, addressed to me at Messrs. Guebhard & Co., merchants, Leghorn: the books may be sent together with it.

Our party at Pisa is the same as when I wrote last. Lord Byron unites us at a weekly dinner, when my nerves are generally shaken to pieces by sitting up contemplating the rest making themselves vats of claret &c. till 3 o'clock in the morning. We regret *your* absence exceedingly, and Lord Byron has desired me to convey his best remembrances to you:—I imagine it is *you* and not your brother for whom they are intended. Hunt was expected, and Lord Byron had fitted up a part of his palace for his accommodation, when we hear that the late violent storms had forced him to put back: and that nothing could induce Marianne to put to sea again. This, for many reasons that I cannot now explain, has produced a chaos of perplexities. . . . . The reviews and journals, they say, continue to attack me, but I value neither the fame they can give nor the fame they can take away, therefore blessed be the name of the reviews.

Pray, if possible, let the "Nympholept" be included in the package.

   Believe me, my dear Smith,
     Your most obliged and
       affectionate friend,
         P. B. SHELLEY.

XLVIII

To LEIGH HUNT.

Pisa, 2nd March, 1822.

MY DEAREST FRIEND,

My last two or three letters have, I fear, given you some uneasiness, or at least inflicted that portion of it which I felt in writing them. The aspect of affairs has somewhat changed since the date of that in which I expressed a repugnance to a continuance of intimacy with Lord Byron, so close as that which now exists; at least, it has been changed so far as regards you and the intended journal. He expresses again the greatest eagerness to undertake it, and proceed with it, as well as the greatest confidence in you as his associate. He is for ever dilating upon his impatience of your delay, and his disappointment at your not having already arrived. He renews his expressions of disregard for the opinion of those who advised him against this alliance with you, and I imagine it will be no very difficult task to execute that which you have assigned me, to keep him in heart with the project until your arrival. Meanwhile, let my last letters, as far as they regard Lord Byron, be as if they had not been written. Particular circumstances, or rather, I should say, particular dispositions in Lord Byron's character, render the close and exclusive intimacy with him in which I find myself intolerable to me; thus much, my best friend, I will confess and confide to you. No feeling of my own shall injure or interfere with what is now nearest to them, your interest, and I will take care to preserve the little influence I may have over this Proteus in whom such strange extremes are reconciled, until we meet, which we now must, at all events, soon do.

Lord Byron showed me your letter to him, which arrived with mine yesterday. How shall I thank you for your generous and delicate defence and explanation of my motives? I fear no misinterpretation from you, and from any one else I despise and defy it.

So you think I can make nothing of "Charles the First." *Tanto peggio.* Indeed, I have written nothing for this last two months; a slight circumstance gave a new train to my ideas, and shattered the fragile edifice when half built. What motives have I to write? I had motives, and I thank the god of my own heart they were totally different from those of the other apes of humanity who make mouths in the glass of the time. But what are those motives now? The only inspiration of an ordinary kind I could descend to acknowledge would be the earning 100*l.* for you; and that it seems I cannot.

Poor Marianne, how ill she seems to have been! Give my best love to her, and tell her I hope she is better, and that I know, as soon as she can resolve to set sail, that she will be better. Your rooms are still ready for you at Lord Byron's. I am afraid they will be rather hot in the summer; they were delightful winter rooms. . . . . . All happiness attend you, my best friend, and believe that I am watching over your interest with the vigilance of painful affection. Mary will write next post. Adieu. Yours,

S.

XLIX

To JOHN GISBORNE.

Pisa, 10th April, 1822.

MY DEAR GISBORNE,

I have received "Hellas," which is prettily printed, and with fewer mistakes than any poem I have ever published. Am I to thank you for the revision of the press? or who acted as midwife to this last of my orphans, introducing it to oblivion, and me to my accustomed failure? May the cause it celebrates be more fortunate than either! Tell me how you like "Hellas," and give me your opinion freely. It was written without much care, and in one of those few moments of enthusiasm which now seldom visit me, and which make me pay dear for their visits. I know what to think of "Adonais," but what to think of those who confound it with the many bad poems of the day, I know not.

I have been reading over and over again "Faust," and always with sensations which no other composition excites. It deepens the gloom and augments the rapidity of ideas, and would therefore seem to me an unfit study for any person who is a prey to the reproaches of memory, and the delusions of an imagination not to be restrained. And yet the pleasure of sympathising with emotions known only to few, although they derive their sole charm from despair, and the scorn of the narrow good we can attain in our present state, seems more than to ease the pain which belongs to them. Perhaps all discontent with the less, to use a Platonic sophism, supposes the sense of a just claim to the greater, and that we admirers of "Faust" are on the right road to paradise. Such a supposition is not more absurd, and is certainly less demoniacal, than that of Wordsworth, where he says—

> " This earth,
> Which is the world of all of us, and where
> We find our happiness, or not at all."

As if, after sixty years' suffering here, we were to be roasted alive for sixty million more in hell, or charitably annihilated by a coup-de-grace of the bungler who brought us into existence at first!

Have you read Calderon's "Magico Prodigioso"? I find a striking similarity between "Faust" and this drama, and if I were to acknowledge Coleridge's distinction, should say Goethe was the greatest philosopher, and Calderon the greatest poet. Cyprian evidently furnished the germ of "Faust," as "Faust" may furnish the germ of other poems; although it is as different from it in structure and plan as the acorn from the oak. I have—imagine my presumption—translated several scenes from both, as the basis of a paper for our journal. I am well content with those from Calderon, which, in fact, gave me very little trouble; but those from "Faust," I feel how imperfect a representation—even with all the license I assume to figure to myself how Goethe would have written in English—my words convey. No one but Coleridge is capable of this work.

We have seen here a translation of some scenes, and indeed the most remarkable ones, accompanying those astonishing etchings which have been published in England from a German master. It is not bad, and faithful enough, but how weak! how incompetent to represent "Faust!" I have only attempted the scenes omitted in this translation, and would send you that of the "Walpurgisnacht," if I thought Ollier would place the postage to my account. What etchings those are! I am never satiated with looking at them; and, I fear, it is the only sort of translation of which "Faust" is susceptible. I never perfectly understood the Hartz mountain scene, until I saw the etching; and then Margaret in the summer-house with Faust! The artist makes one envy his happiness that he can sketch such things with calmness, which I only dared look upon once, and which made my brain swim round only to touch the leaf on the opposite side of which I knew that it was figured. Whether it is that the artist has surpassed "Faust," or that the pencil surpasses language in some subjects, I know not, or that I am more affected by a visible image, but the etching certainly excited me far more than the poem it illustrated. Do you remember the fifty-fourth letter of the first part of the "Nouvelle Héloïse"? Goethe, in a subsequent scene, evidently had that letter in his mind, and this etching is an idealism of it. So much for the world of shadows!

What think you of Lord Byron's last volume? In my opinion it contains finer poetry than has appeared in England since the publication of "Paradise Regained." "Cain" is apocalyptic, it is a revelation not before communicated to man. I write nothing but by fits. I have done some of "Charles I."; but although the poetry succeeded very well, I cannot seize on the conception of the subject as a whole, and seldom now touch the canvas. You know I don't think much about reviews, nor of the fame they give, nor that they take away. It is absurd in any review to criticise "Adonais," and still more to pretend that the verses are bad. "Prometheus" was never intended for more than five or six persons.

And how are you getting on ? Do your plans still want success ? Do you regret Italy ? or anything that Italy contains ? and in case of an entire failure in your expectations, do you think of returning here ? You see the first blow has been made at funded property: do you intend to confide and invite a second ? You would already have saved something per cent. if you had invested your property in Tuscan land. The best next thing would be to invest it in English, and reside upon it. I tremble for the consequences, to you personally, from a prolonged confidence in the funds. Justice, policy, the hopes of the nation and renewed institutions, demand your ruin, and I for one cannot bring myself to desire what is in itself desirable, till you are free. You see how liberal I am of advice ; but you know the motives that suggest it. What is Henry about, and how are his prospects ? Tell him that some adventurers are engaged upon a steam-boat at Leghorn to make the *trajet* we projected. I hope he is charitable enough to pray that they may succeed better than we did.

* * * * * *

Remember me most affectionately to Mrs. Gisborne, to whom, as well as to yourself, I consider that this letter is written. How is she, and how are you all in health? and pray tell me what are your plans of life, and how Henry succeeds, and whether he is married or not? How can I send you such small sums as you may want for postages, etc.? for I do not mean to tax with my unreasonable letters both your purse and your patience. We go this summer to Spezzia; but direct as ever to Pisa; Mrs. Mason will forward our letters. If you see anything which you think would particularly interest me, pray make Ollier pay for sending it out by the post. Give my best and affectionate regards to Hogg, to whom I do not write at present, imagining that you will give him a piece of this letter.

Ever most faithfully yours,
P. B. S.

L

To HORACE SMITH.

Pisa, April 11, 1822.

MY DEAR SMITH,

I have, as yet, received neither the "Nympholept," nor his metaphysical companions. *Time, my lord, has a wallet on his back*, and I suppose he has bagged them by the way. As he has had a good deal of alms for oblivion out of me, I think he might as well have favoured me this once; I have, indeed, just dropped another mite into his treasury, called "Hellas," which I know not how to send to you; but I dare say some fury of the Hades of authors will bring one to Paris. It is a poem written on the Greek cause last summer, a sort of lyrical, dramatic, nondescript piece of business.

You will have heard of a row we have had here, which, I dare say, will grow to a serious size before it arrives at Paris. It was, in fact, a trifling piece of business enough, arising from an insult of a drunken dragoon, offered to one of our party, and only serious, because one of Lord Byron's servants wounded the fellow dangerously with a pitchfork. He is now, however, recover-

ing, and the echo of the affair will be heard long
after the original report has ceased.

Lord Byron has read me one or two letters of
Moore to him, in which Moore speaks with great
kindness of me ; and, of course, I cannot but feel
flattered by the approbation of a man, my in-
feriority to whom I am proud to acknowledge.
Amongst other things, however, Moore, after
giving Lord Byron much good advice about public
opinion, etc., seems to deprecate my influence
over his mind on the subject of religion, and to
attribute the tone assumed in " Cain " to my
suggestions. Moore cautions him against my
influence on this particular, with the most friendly
zeal ; and it is plain that his motive springs from
a desire of benefiting Lord Byron without degrading me. I think you know Moore. Pray assure
him that I have not the smallest influence over
Lord Byron in this particular, and if I had, I
certainly should employ it to eradicate from his
great mind the delusions of Christianity, which,
in spite of his reason, seem perpetually to recur,
and to lay in ambush for the hours of sickness
and distress. " Cain " was conceived many years
ago, and begun before I saw him last year at
Ravenna. How happy should I not be to attribute to myself, however indirectly, any participa-

tion in that immortal work! I differ with Moore in thinking Christianity useful to the world; no man of sense can think it true; and the alliance of the monstrous superstitions of the popular worship with the pure doctrines of the theism of such men as Moore, turns to the profit of the former, and but makes the latter the fountain of its own pollution. I agree with him that the doctrines of the French, and material philosophy are as false as they are pernicious; but still they are better than Christianity, inasmuch as anarchy is better than despotism; for this reason, that the former is for a season, and that the latter is eternal. My admiration of the character, no less than of the genius of Moore, makes me rather wish that he should not have an ill opinion of me.

Where are you this summer? For ever in Paris? For ever in France? May I not hope to see you, even for a trip, in Italy? How is Mrs. Smith? I hope she finds the air of France propitious to her health, and that your little ones are well . . . . Mine grows a fine boy, and is quite well . . . .

I have contrived to get my musical coals at Newcastle itself. My dear Smith, believe me,

Most faithfully yours,
P. B. S.

LI

To JOHN GISBORNE.

Lerici, June 18, 1822.

In my doubt as to which of your most interesting letters I shall answer, I quash the business one for the present, as the only part of it that requires an answer requires also mature consideration. In the first place I send you money for postage, as I intend to indulge myself in plenty of paper and no crossings. Mary will write soon; at present she suffers greatly from excess of weakness, produced by a severe miscarriage, from which she is now slowly recovering. Her situation for some hours was alarming, and as she was totally destitute of medical assistance I took the most decisive resolutions, and by dint of making her sit in ice, I succeeded in checking the hemorrhage and the fainting fits, so that when the physician arrived all danger was over, and he had nothing to do but to applaud me for my boldness. She is now doing well, and the sea-baths will soon restore her. I have written to Ollier to send his account to you. The "Adonais" I wished to have had a fair chance, both because it was a favourite with me, and on account of the memory of Keats, who was a poet of great genius, let the classic party say what it will. "Hellas" too I liked on account of the subject, one always finds some reason or other for liking one's own composition. The "Epipsychidion" I cannot look at; the person whom it celebrates was a cloud instead of a Juno; and poor Ixion starts from the Centaur that was the offspring of his own embrace. If you are curious, however, to hear what I am and have been, it will tell you something thereof. It is an idealized history of my life and feelings. I think one is always in love with something or other; the error, and I confess it is not easy for spirits cased in flesh and blood to avoid it, consists in seeking in a mortal image the likeness of what is, perhaps, eternal.

Hunt is not yet arrived, but I expect him every day. I shall see little of Lord Byron, nor shall I permit Hunt to form the intermediate link between him and me. I detest all society—almost all, at least—and Lord Byron is the nucleus of all that is hateful and tiresome in it. He will be half mad to hear of these memoirs. As to me, you know my supreme indifference to such affairs, except that I must confess I am sometimes amused by the ridiculous mistakes of these writers. Tell me a little what they say of me besides being an atheist. One thing I regret in it, I dread lest it should

injure Hunt's prospects in the establishment of the
journal, for Lord Byron is so mentally capricious
that the least impulse drives him from his anchor-
age. The Williamses are now on a visit to us,
and they are people who are very pleasing to me.
But words are not the instruments of our intercourse. I like Jane more and more, and I find
Williams the most amiable of companions. She
has a taste for music, and an elegance of form and
motions that compensate in some degree for the
lack of literary refinement. You know my gross
ideas of music, and will forgive me when I say
that I listen the whole evening on our terrace to
the simple melodies with excessive delight. I have
a boat here. It cost me 80*l.*, and reduced me
to some difficulty in point of money. However,
it is swift and beautiful, and appears quite a vessel.
Williams is captain, and we drive along in this
delightful bay in the evening wind under the summer moon until earth appears another world. Jane
brings her guitar, and if the past and the future
could be obliterated, the present would content me
so well that I could say with Faust to the passing
moment, "Remain thou, thou art so beautiful."
Claire is with us, and the death of her child seems
to have restored her to tranquillity. Her character
is somewhat altered. She is vivacious and talka-

tive; and though she teases me sometimes, I like her. .... Lord Byron, who is at Leghorn, has fitted up a splendid vessel, a small schooner on the American model, and Trelawny is to be captain. How long the fiery spirit of our pirate will accommo_ date itself to the caprice of the poet remains to be seen. ....

I write little now. It is impossible to compose except under the strong excitement of an assurance of finding sympathy in what you write. Imagine Demosthenes reciting a Philippic to the waves of the Atlantic. Lord Byron is in this respect fortunate. He touched the chord to which a million hearts responded, and the coarse music which he produced to please them, disciplined him to the perfection to which he now approaches. I do not go on with " Charles the First." I feel too little certainty of the future, and too little satisfaction with regard to the past to undertake any subject seriously and deeply. I stand, as it were, upon a precipice, which I have ascended with great, and cannot descend without greater peril, and I am content if the heaven above me is calm for the passing moment.

You don't tell me what you think of "Cain." You send me the opinion of the populace, which you know I do not esteem. I have read several more of the plays of Calderon. " Los Dos Amantes del

Cielo" is the finest, if I except one scene in the
"Devocion de la Cruz." I read Greek, and think
about writing.

I do not think much of Emma's not admiring Metastasio; the *Nil admirari*, however justly applied, seems to me a bad sign in a young person. I had rather a pupil of mine had conceived a frantic passion for Marini himself than that she had found out the critical defects of the most deficient author. When she becomes of her own accord full of genuine admiration for the finest scene in the "Purgatorio," or the opening of the "Paradiso," or some other neglected piece of excellence, hope great things. Adieu, I must not exceed the limits of my paper, however little scrupulous I seem about those of your patience.

P. B. S.

I waited three days to get this pen mended, and at last was obliged to write.

LII

To HORACE SMITH.

Lerici, June 29, 1822.

MY DEAR SMITH,

Pray thank Moore for his obliging message. I wish I could as easily convey my sense of his genius and character. I should have written to him on the subject of my late letter, but that I doubted how far I was justified in doing so; although, indeed, Lord Byron made no secret of his communication to me. It seems to me that things have now arrived at such a crisis as requires every man plainly to utter his sentiments on the inefficiency of the existing religious, no less than political systems, for restraining and guiding mankind. Let us see the truth, whatever that may be. The destiny of man can scarcely be so degraded, that he was born only to die; and if such should be the case, delusions, especially the gross and preposterous ones of the existing religion, can scarcely be supposed to exalt it. If every man said what he thought, it could not subsist a day. But all, more or less, subdue themselves to the element that surrounds them, and contribute to the evils they lament by the hypocrisy that springs from them.

England appears to be in a desperate condition, Ireland still worse ; and no class of those who subsist on the public labour will be persuaded that their claims on it must be diminished. But the government must content itself with less in taxes, the landowner must submit to receive less rent, and the fundholder a diminished interest, or they will all get nothing or something worse than nothing. I once thought to study these affairs, and write or act in them. I am glad that my good genius said Refrain. I see little public virtue, and I foresee that the contest will be one of blood and gold, two elements which, however much to my taste in my pockets and my veins, I have an objection to out of them.

Lord Byron continues at Leghorn, and has just received from Genoa a most beautiful little yacht, which he caused to be built there. He has written two new cantos of " Don Juan," but I have not seen them. I have just received a letter from Hunt, who has arrived at Genoa. As soon as I hear that he has sailed, I shall weigh anchor in my little schooner, and give him chase to Leghorn, where I must occupy myself in some arrangements for him with Lord Byron. Between ourselves, I greatly fear that this alliance will not succeed, for I, who could never have been regarded more than the link of the two thunderbolts, cannot now consent to be even that; and how long the alliance between the wren and the eagle may continue, I will not prophesy. Pray do not hint my doubts on the subject to any one, as they might do harm to Hunt; and they may be groundless.

I still inhabit this divine bay, reading Spanish dramas, and sailing and listening to the most enchanting music. We have some friends on a visit to us, and my only regret is that the summer must ever pass, or that Mary has not the same predilection for this place that I have, which would induce me never to shift my quarters.

Farewell,—believe me ever your
Obliged and affectionate friend,
P. B. SHELLEY.

LIII

To Mrs. Williams.

Pisa, July 4, 1822.

You will probably see Williams before I can disentangle myself from the affairs with which I am now surrounded. I return to Leghorn tonight, and shall urge him to sail with the first fair wind, without expecting me. I have thus the pleasure of contributing to your happiness when deprived of every other, and of leaving you no other subject of regret, but the absence of one scarcely worth regretting. I fear you are solitary and melancholy at Villa Magni, and, in the intervals of the greater and more serious distress in which I am compelled to sympathize here, I figure to myself the countenance which has been the source of such consolation to me, shadowed by a veil of sorrow.

How soon those hours passed, and how slowly they return, to pass so soon again, and perhaps for ever, in which we have lived together so intimately and happily! Adieu, my dearest friend. I only write these lines for the pleasure of tracing what will meet your eyes. Mary will tell you all the news.

S.

LETTER FROM
MRS. SHELLEY TO MRS. GISBORNE.

August 15th, 1822.

I said in a letter to Peacock, my dear Mrs. Gisborne, that I would send you some account of the last miserable months of my disastrous life. From day to day I have put this off, but I will now endeavour to fulfil my design. The scene of my existence is closed, and though there be no pleasure in retracing the scenes that have preceded the event which has crushed my hopes, yet there seems to be a necessity in doing so, and I obey the impulse that urges me.

I wrote to you either at the end of May or the beginning of June. I described to you the place we were living in, our desolate house, the beauty yet strangeness of the scenery, and the delight Shelley took in all this: he never was in better health or spirits than during this time. I was not well in body or mind. My nerves were wound up to the utmost irritation, and the sense of misfortune hung over my spirits. No words can tell you how I hated our house and the country about it. Shelley reproached me for this; his health was good, and the place was quite after his own heart. What could I answer? That the people were wild and hateful; that, though the country was beautiful, yet I like a more *countryfied* place? that there was great difficulty in living; that all our Tuscans would leave us, and that the very jargon of these Genoese was disgusting.

This was all I had to say, but no words could describe my feelings; the beauty of the woods made me weep and shudder: so vehement was my feeling of dislike that I used to rejoice when the winds and waves permitted me to go out in the boat, so that I was not obliged to take my usual walk among tree-shaded paths, alleys of vine-festooned trees—all that before I doated on: and that now weighed on me. My only moments of peace were on board that unhappy boat when, lying down with my head on his knee, I shut my eyes, and felt the wind and our swift motion alone.

My ill-health might account for much of this; bathing in the sea somewhat relieved me: but on the 8th of June, I think it was, I was threatened with a miscarriage, and, after a week of great ill-health, on Sunday the 16th this took place at eight in the morning. I was so ill that for seven hours I lay nearly lifeless—kept from fainting by brandy, vinegar, eau-de-Cologne, etc. At length ice was brought to our solitude : it came before the doctor, so Claire and Jane were afraid of using it ; but Shelley overruled them, and by an unsparing application of it I was restored. They all thought, and so did I at one time, that I was about to die. I hardly wish that I had ; my own Shelley could never have lived without me, the sense of eternal misfortune would have pressed too heavily upon him, and what would have become of my poor babe ? My convalescence was slow, and during it a strange occurrence happened to retard it.

But first I must describe our house to you. The floor on which we lived was thus—

5	7		3
6	2		4
	1		

1 is a terrace that went the whole length of our house, and was precipitous to the sea; 2 the large dining hall; 3 a private staircase; 4 my bedroom; 5 Mrs. Williams's bedroom; 6 Shelley's; and 7 the entrance from the great staircase.

Now to return. As I said, Shelley was at first in perfect health, but having over-fatigued himself one day, and then the fright my illness gave him, caused a return of nervous sensations, and visions as bad as in his worst times. I think it was the Saturday after my illness, while, yet unable to walk, I was confined to my bed. In the middle of the night I was awoke by hearing him scream, and come rushing into my room. I was sure that he was asleep, and tried to wake him by calling on him; but he continued to scream, which inspired me with such a panic that I jumped out of bed, and ran across the hall to Mrs. Williams's room, where I fell through weakness, though I was so frightened that I got up again immediately. She let me in, and Williams went to Shelley, who had been awakened by my getting out of bed. He said that he had not been asleep, and that it was a vision that he saw that had frightened him. But as he declared that he had not screamed it was certainly a dream and no waking vision.

What had frightened him was this: He dreamt that, lying as he did in bed, Edward and Jane came in to him; they were in the most horrible condition, their bodies lacerated, their bones starting through their skin, their faces pale yet stained with blood; they could hardly walk, but Edward was the weakest, and Jane was supporting him. Edward said, "Get up, Shelley, the sea is flooding the house, and it is all coming down." Shelley got up, he thought, and went to his window that looked on the terrace and the sea, and thought he saw the sea rushing in. Suddenly his vision changed, and he saw the figure of himself strangling me; that had made him rush into my room, yet, fearful of frightening me, he dared not approach the bed, when my jumping out awoke him, or, as he phrased it, caused his vision to vanish. All this was frightful enough, and talking it over the next morning he told me that he had had many visions lately. He had seen the figure of himself, which met him as he walked on the terrace, and said to him, "How long do you mean to be content?"—no very terrific words, and certainly not prophetic of what has occurred.

But Shelley had often seen these figures when ill; but the strangest thing is that Mrs. Williams saw *him*. Now Jane, although a woman of sensibility, has not much imagination, and is not in the slightest degree nervous, either in dreams or otherwise. She was standing one day, the day before I was taken ill, at a window that looked on the terrace, with Trelawny. It was day; she saw, as she thought, Shelley pass by the window, as he often was then, without a coat or jacket. He passed again. Now as he passed both times the same way, and as from the side towards which he went each time there was no way to get back except past the window again, except over a wall twenty feet from the ground, she was struck at her seeing him pass twice thus, and looked out; and seeing him no more, she cried, " Good God! can Shelley have leapt from the wall? Where can he be gone?" "Shelley!" said Trelawny, " no Shelley has passed. What do you mean?" Trelawny says that she trembled exceedingly when she heard this, and it proved indeed that Shelley had never been on the terrace, and was far off at the time she saw him. Well, we thought no more of these things, and I slowly got better.

Having heard from Hunt that he had sailed from Genoa on Monday July 1st, Shelley, Edward, and Captain Roberts, the gentleman who built our boat, departed in our boat for Leghorn to receive him. I was then just better, had begun to crawl from my bedroom to the terrace, but bad spirits succeeded to ill-health, and this departure of Shelley's seemed to add insufferably to my misery. I could not endure that he should go. I called him back two or three times, and told him that if I did not see him soon I would go to Pisa with the child. I cried bitterly when he went away. They went, and Jane, Claire, and I remained alone with the children. I could not walk out, and though I gradually gathered strength, it was slowly, and my ill spirits increased. In my letters to him I entreated him to return. "The feeling that some misfortune would happen," I said, "haunted me." I feared for the child, for the idea of danger connected with him never struck me.

When Jane and Claire took their evening walk I used to patrole the terrace, oppressed with wretchedness, yet gazing on the most beautiful scene in the world. This Gulf of Spezzia is subdivided into many small bays, of which ours was far the most beautiful; the two horns of the bay, so to express myself, were wood-covered promontories crowned with castles. At the foot of these on the furthest was Lerici, on the nearest San Terenzo, Lerici being above a mile by land from us, and San Terenzo about a hundred or two yards. Trees covered the hills that enclosed this bay, and their beautiful groups were picturesquely contrasted with the rocks, the castle, and the town. The sea lay far extended in front, while to the west we saw the promontory and islands which formed one of the extreme boundaries of the Gulf. To see the sun set upon this scene, the stars shine, and the moon rise, was a sight of wondrous beauty; but to me it added only to my wretchedness. I repeated to myself all that another would have said to console me, and told myself the tale of love, peace, and competence which I enjoyed. But I answered myself by tears—did not my William die? And did I hold my Percy by a firmer tenure? Yet I thought when he, when my Shelley, returns, I shall be happy. He will comfort me, if my boy be ill he will restore him and encourage me.

I had a letter or two from Shelley mentioning the difficulties he had in establishing the Hunts, and that he was unable to fix the time of his return. Thus a week passed. On Monday 8th Jane had a letter from Edward, dated Saturday: he said that he waited at Leghorn for Shelley, who was at Pisa; that Shelley's return was certain; " but," he continued, " if he should not come by

Monday, I will come in a felucca, and you may expect me Tuesday evening at furthest."

This was Monday, the fatal Monday, but with us it was stormy all day, and we did not at all suppose that they could put to sea. At twelve at night we had a thunderstorm, Tuesday it rained all day and was calm—wept on their graves. On Wednesday the wind was fair from Leghorn, and in the evening several feluccas arrived thence. One brought word that they had sailed on Monday, but we did not believe them. Thursday was another day of fair wind, and when twelve at night came, and we did not see the tall sails of the little boat double the promontory before us, we began to fear, not the truth, but some illness, some disagreeable news for their detention.

Jane got so uneasy, that she determined to proceed the next day to Leghorn in a boat to see what was the matter. Friday came, and with it a heavy sea and bad wind. Jane however resolved to be rowed to Leghorn, since no boat could sail, and busied herself in preparations. I wished her to wait for letters, since Friday was letter day. She would not, but the sea detained her; the swell rose so that no boat would venture out. At twelve at noon our letters came; there was one from Hunt to Shelley; it said, " Pray write to tell us how you got home, for they say that you had bad weather after you sailed on Monday, and we are anxious." The paper fell from me. I trembled all over. Jane read it. "Then it is all over!" she said. "No, my dear Jane," I cried, "it is not all over, but this suspense is dreadful. Come with me, we will go to Leghorn, we will post to be swift, and learn our fate."

We crossed to Lerici, despair in our hearts; they raised our spirits there by telling us that no accident had been heard of, and that it must have been known, etc. But still our fear was great, and without resting we posted to Pisa. It must have been fearful to see us—two poor, wild, aghast creatures—driving, like Matilda, towards the sea to learn if we were to be for ever doomed to misery. I knew that Hunt was at Pisa at Lord Byron's house, but I thought that Lord Byron was at Leghorn. I settled that we should drive to Casa Lanfranchi, that I should get out and ask the fearful question of Hunt, "Do you know anything of Shelley?" On entering Pisa the idea of seeing Hunt for the first time for four years under such circumstances, and asking him such a question, was so terrific to me, that it was with difficulty that I prevented myself from going into convulsions. My struggles were dreadful. They

knocked at the door, and some one called out
"Chi è?" It was the Guiccioli's maid. Lord
Byron was in Pisa. Hunt was in bed, so I was
to see Lord Byron instead of him. This was a
great relief to me; I staggered up stairs; the
Guiccioli came to meet me smiling, while I could
hardly say, "Where is he—Sapete alcuna cosa di
Shelley?" They knew nothing; he had left Pisa
on Sunday; on Monday he had sailed; there had
been bad weather Monday afternoon; more they
knew not.

Both Lord Byron and the lady have told me since
that on that terrific evening I looked more like a
ghost than a woman; light seemed to emanate from
my features, my face was very white, I looked
like marble. Alas, I had risen almost from a bed
of sickness for this journey. I had travelled all
day; it was now twelve at night, and we, re-
fusing to rest, proceeded to Leghorn—not in despair—no, for then we must have died, but with
sufficient hope to keep up the agitation of the
spirits which was all my life. It was past two
in the morning when we arrived. They took
us to the wrong inn; neither Trelawny or Captain Roberts were there, nor did we exactly know
where they were, so we were obliged to wait
until daylight. We threw ourselves drest on

our beds, and slept a little, but at six o'clock we went to one or two inns to ask for one or the other of these gentlemen. We found Roberts at the Globe. He came down to us with a face which seemed to tell us that the worst was true, and here we learned all that had occurred during the week they had been absent from us, and under what circumstances they had departed on their return.

Shelley had passed most of the time at Pisa, arranging the affairs of the Hunts, and screwing Lord Byron's mind to the sticking place about the journal. He had found this a difficult task at first, but at length he had succeeded to his heart's content with both points. Mrs. Mason said that she saw him in better health and spirits than she had ever known him, when he took leave of her Sunday July 7th, his face burnt by the sun, and his heart light that he had succeeded in rendering the Hunts tolerably comfortable. Edward had remained at Leghorn. On Monday, July 8th, during the morning they were employed in buying many things—eatables, etc., for our solitude. There had been a thunderstorm early, but about noon the weather was fine, and the wind right fair for Lerici. They were impatient to be gone. Roberts said, "Stay until to-morrow to see if the weather is settled ;" and Shelley might have stayed, but Edward was in so great an anxiety to reach home—saying they would get there in seven hours with that wind —that they sailed, Shelley being in one of those extravagant fits of good spirits in which you have sometimes seen him. Roberts went out to the end of the mole and watched them out of sight. They sailed at once, and went off at the rate of about seven knots. About three, Roberts, who was still on the mole, saw wind coming from the Gulf, or rather what the Italians call a *temporale*. Anxious to know how the boat would weather the storm, he got leave to go up the tower, and with the glass discovered them about ten miles out at sea, off Via Reggio; they were taking in their topsails. "The haze of the storm," he said, "hid them from me, and I saw them no more. When the storm cleared I looked again, fancying that I should see them on their return to us, but there was no boat on the sea."

This then was all we knew, yet we did not despair; they might have been driven over to Corsica, and, not knowing the coast, have gone God knows where. Reports favoured this belief. It was even said that they had been seen in the Gulf. I resolved to return with all possible speed; we sent a courier to go from tower to tower along the coast to know if anything had been seen or found, and at nine A.M. we quitted Leghorn, stopped but one moment at Pisa, and proceeded towards Lerici. When at two miles from Via Reggio we rode down to that town to know if they knew anything. Here our calamity first began to break on us. A little boat and a water cask had been found five miles off. They had manufactured a *piccolissima lancia* of thin planks stitched by a shoemaker, just to let them run on shore without wetting themselves, as our boat drew four feet of water. The description of that found tallied with this, but then this boat was very cumbersome, and in bad weather they might have been easily led to throw it overboard. The cask frightened me most, but the same reason might in some sort be given for that. I must tell you that Jane and I were not now alone. Trelawny accompanied us back to our home. We journeyed on and reached the Magra about half-past ten P.M. I cannot describe to you what I felt in the first moment when, fording this river, I felt the water splash about our wheels. I was suffocated. I gasped for breath. I thought I should have gone into convulsions, and I struggled violently that Jane might not perceive it. Looking down the river I saw the two great lights burning at the *foce*: a voice from within me seemed to cry aloud, That is his grave.

After passing the river I gradually recovered. Arriving at Lerici we were obliged to cross our little bay in a boat. San Terenzo was illuminated for a festa. What a scene ı The waving sea, the scirocco wind, the lights of the town towards which we rowed, and our own desolate hearts, that coloured all with a shroud. We landed; nothing had been heard of them. This was Saturday, July 13, and thus we waited until Thursday, July 25th, thrown about by hope and fear. We sent passengers along the coast towards Genoa and to Via Reggio — nothing had been found more than the *lancetta*. Reports were brought us: we hoped; and yet to tell you all the agony we endured during those twelve days would be to make you conceive a universe of pain, each moment intolerable, and giving place to one still worse. The people of the country too added to one's discomfort; they are like wild savages. On festas the men and women and children in different bands—the sexes always separate—pass the whole night in dancing on the sands close to our door, running into the sea, then back again, and screaming all the time one perpetual air—the most detestable in the world. Then the scirocco perpetually blew, and the sea for ever moaned their dirge. On Thursday 25th Trelawny left us to go to Leghorn to see what was doing, or what could be done. On Friday I was very ill, but as evening came on I said to Jane, "If anything had been found on the coast Trelawny would have returned to let us know. He has not returned, so I hope." About seven o'clock P.M. he did return. All was over: all was quiet now; they had been found washed on shore. Well, all this was to be endured.

Well, what more have I to say? The next day we returned to Pisa, and here we are still. Days pass away, one after another, and we live thus. We are all together—we shall quit Italy together. Jane must proceed to London. If letters do not alter my views I shall remain in Paris. Thus we live, seeing the Hunts now and then. Poor Hunt has suffered terribly, as you may guess. Lord Byron is very kind to me, and comes with the Guiccioli to see me often. To-day—this day—the sun shining in the sky—they are gone to the desolate sea-coast to perform the last offices to their earthly remains, Hunt, Lord Byron, and Trelawny. The quarantine laws would not permit us to remove them sooner, and now only on condition that we burn them to ashes. That I do not dislike. His rest shall be at Rome beside my child, where one day I also shall join them. "Adonais" is not Keats's; it is his own elegy. He bids you there go to Rome. I have seen the spot where he now lies, the sticks that mark the spot where the sands cover him. He shall not be there, it is too near Via Reggio. They are now about this fearful office—and I live.

One more circumstance I will mention. As I said, he took leave of Mrs. Mason in high spirits on Sunday. "Never," said she, "did I see him look happier than the last glance I had of his countenance." On Monday he was lost; on Monday night she dreamt that she was somewhere, she knew not where, and he came looking very pale, and fearfully melancholy. She said to him, "You look ill, you are tired, sit down and eat." "No," he replied, "I shall never eat more, I have not a soldo left in the world." "Nonsense," said she, "this is no inn, you need not pay." "Perhaps," he answered, "it is the worse for that." Then she awoke, and going to sleep again she dreamt that my Percy was dead, and she awoke crying bitterly, so bitterly and felt so miserable, that she said to herself, "Why, if the little boy should die I should not feel it in this manner." She was so struck with these dreams, that she mentioned them to her servant the next day, saying she hoped all was well with us.

Well, here is my story—the last story I shall have to tell. All that might have been bright in my life is now despoiled. I shall live to improve myself, to take care of my child, and render myself worthy to join *him*. Soon my weary pilgrimage will begin. I rest now, but soon I must leave Italy, and then—there is an end of all but despair. Adieu! I hope you are well and happy. I have an idea that while he was at Pisa he received a letter from you that I have never seen, so not knowing where to direct I shall send this letter to Peacock. I shall send it open; he may be glad to read it.

Yours ever truly,
Mary W. S.

Pisa, 15th August, 1822.

I shall probably write to you soon again. I have left out a material circumstance. A fishing boat saw them go down. It was about four in the afternoon. They saw the boy at mast-head, when baffling winds struck the sails. They had looked away a moment, and looking again the boat was gone. This is their story, but there is little doubt that these men might have saved them, at least

Edward, who could swim. They could not, they said, get near her, but three quarters of an hour after passed over the spot where they had seen her. They protested no wreck of her was visible, but Roberts going on board their boat found several spars belonging to her. Perhaps they let them perish to obtain these. Trelawny thinks he can get her up, since another fisherman thinks that he has found the spot where she lies, having drifted near shore. Trelawny does this to know perhaps the cause of her wreck, but I care little about it.

NOTES.

P. 10, *l.* 19. *"Southey calls himself a Christian,"* etc. Shelley undoubtedly misinterpreted Southey's views; it is nevertheless evident that Southey's subsequent statement that he avoided discussion with him upon religious subjects must be received with some qualification. For this statement, and for Southey's feelings towards Shelley in general, see the letters between them published by Professor Dowden. *(Correspondence of Robert Southey with Caroline Bowles.)*

P. 11, *l.* 13. *"With Calvert."* Mr. Calvert, of Greta Bank, near Keswick. He was no doubt a relation of Raisley Calvert, Wordsworth's benefactor, and may have been the William Calvert in whose company Wordsworth visited the Isle of Wight in 1793. "The Duke [of Norfolk] and his friends were very fond of him; he promoted all local improvements, and was a person of great vigour and originality of mind."—Mr. P. H. Howard in "Shelley's Early Life," by D. F. MacCarthy, pp. 137, 138.

P. 13, *l.* 11. *"You talk of Montgomery.... His story is a terrible one."* The story here narrated seems to have no other foundation than the circumstance of Montgomery's parents, who were missionaries, having died in the West Indies, within eight months of each other, of diseases incident to the climate.

P. 15, *l.* 4. The party on this expedition consisted of Shelley, Mrs. Shelley, Peacock, and Charles Clairmont, the second Mrs. Godwin's son by a former marriage. "Our voyage," Peacock says, "terminated at a spot where the cattle stood entirely across the stream, with the water scarcely covering their hoofs." According to Charles Clairmont, Shelley wished to take the boat through a canal into the Severn, and so into the heart of Wales, but the heavy lock charges effectually discouraged the project. It bore fruit, however, in "Crotchet Castle," where such a navigation is an incident in the story. Shelley's "Lines in Lechlade Churchyard" were written on this occasion.

P. 15, *l.* 8. "*So favourable an effect on my health.*" This improvement is attributed by Peacock to the magic effect on the vegetarian of "three mutton chops, well peppered."

P. 16, *l.* 1. "*Lucan's 'Pharsalia,' a poem, as it appears to me, of wonderful genius, and transcending Virgil.*" Southey thought much the same: "The ill-chosen subjects of Lucan and Statius have prevented them from acquiring the popularity they would otherwise have merited, yet in detached parts the former is perhaps unequalled, certainly unexcelled. I do not scruple to prefer Statius to Virgil."—*Preface to "Joan of Arc."*

P. 28, *l.* 14. "*A tragedy on the subject of Tasso's madness.*" One scene and one song for this projected drama have been printed in Shelley's works. The following notes for intended scenes have not hitherto been published:—"Scene where he reads the sonnet which he wrote to Leonora to herself as composed at the request of another.—His disguising himself in the habit of a shepherd, and questioning his sister in that disguise concerning himself, and then unveiling himself."

P. 28, at bottom. *"You tell me nothing of Rhododaphne."* "Rhododaphne, or The Thessalian Spell," was a poem by Peacock of very considerable merit, of which Shelley wrote a review, apparently intended for the *Examiner*, but not then published. It has been printed by Mr. Forman, who points out that Edgar Poe also thought highly of "Rhododaphne."

P. 34, l. 3. *"To venture an unrhythmical paraphrase."* "The reference is to the third stanza of Wordsworth's beautiful poem 'The Thorn,' as printed in the editions current in Shelley's time."—*Forman.*

P. 37, l. 13. *"The little poem."* "Rosalind and Helen."

P. 38, l. 19. *"Even when the nymph is a Poliad."* Peacock says: "I suppose I understood this at the time, but I have not now the most distant recollection of what it alludes to."

P. 38, last line. *"What a wonderful passage there is in Phaedrus."* Thus rendered by Peacock:—"There are several kinds of divine madness. That which proceeds from the Muses' taking possession of a tender and unoccupied soul, awakening and bacchically inspiring it towards songs and other poetry, adorning myriads of ancient deeds, instructs succeeding generations; but he who without this madness from the Muses, approaches the poetical gates, having persuaded himself that by art alone he may become sufficiently a poet, will find in the end his own imperfection, and see the poetry of his cold prudence vanish into nothingness before the light of that which has sprung from divine insanity."

P. 42, three lines from bottom. "*Such fruits of my absence.*" "*Frankenstein.*"

P. 54, l. 7-9. "*Usually flattened by a broken column.*" "Area cum primis ingenti aequanda cylindro."—Virg. Georg. I. 178. "Pro cylindro rotundum lapidem *vel columnae fragmentum* memorat Palladius." Heyne's note on the passage—An interesting proof of the late period of Palladius, and of the condition of Italy in his time.—— "*Neither the mole, the toad, nor the ant*":

"Tum variae inludunt pestes; saepe exiguus mus
Sub terris posuitque domos atque horrea fecit;
Aut oculis capti fodere cubilia talpae,
Inventusque cavis bufo, et quae plurima terrae.
Monstra ferunt, populatque ingentem farris acervum
Curculio, atque inopi metuens formica senectae."

vv. 181-185.

P. 57, l. 4. "*How it applies to Ariosto, I cannot exactly tell.*" "The motto of this medal [by Poggini] is the same as that on the medal of Ariosto by Pastorini of Siena. But the meaning of the reverse design is very different. Both, it is probable, refer to the quarrel between Ariosto and the elder Cardinal d'Este; but one takes the side of the poet, who is symbolised by the bees, expelled from their home as an ungrateful return for the honey which they have given ; while the other medal, taking the side of Cardinal d'Este, symbolises Ariosto as a serpent who stings those that have nurtured him."— *Guide to the Italian Medals exhibited in the British Museum,* by C. F. Keary.

P. 59, *l.* 6. "*Seven years and three months.*" Tasso's confinement in this cell, if he was confined in it at all, only continued from March, 1579, to December, 1580.

P. 65, *l.* 17. "*Franceschini.*" The last painter of the Bolognese school (1648–1729).

P. 73, *l.* 21. "*The castle was built by Belisarius or Narses.*" It was built by Theodoric, rebuilt by Narses, restored by Cardinal Albornoz, and enlarged by Pope Nicholas V.

P. 86, *l.* 4. "*In the 'Civil War' of Petronius.*" The passage is as follows :

"Est locus, exciso penitus demersus hiatu,
Parthenopen inter magnaeque Dicarchidos arva,
Cocyta perfusus aqua ; nam spiritus extra
Qui furit, effusus funesto spargitur aestu.
Non haec autumno tellus viret, aut alit herbas
Cespite laetus ager ; non verno persona cantu,
Mollia discordi strepitu virgulta loquuntur.
Sed chaos, et nigro squallentia pumice saxa
Gaudent ferali circum tumulata cupressu."

P. 93, *l.* 5. "*That balance which the giant of Arthegall holds.*" "The allusion is to the 'Faery Queen,' book v. canto 3."—*Peacock.*

P. 100, *l.* 20. "*Like the step of ghosts.*" The same comparison is made in the "Ode to the West Wind," "The Sensitive Plant," and the "Ode to Naples."

P. 102, *l.* 3. "*Your removal to London.*" On becoming an assistant examiner at the India House.

P. 107, *l.* 21. "*These columns do not seem more than forty feet high.*" "The height of the columns is respectively 18 feet 6 inches, and 28 feet 5 inches and 6½ lines, in the first two temples; and 21 feet 6 inches in the Basilica. This shows the justice of the remarks on the difference of real and apparent magnitude."—*Peacock.*

P. 122, at bottom. "*Above these are the niches,*" etc. It has recently been proved that the Pantheon was originally intended for a colossal hot-air bath, and that these recesses were connected with the apparatus.

P. 138, *l.* 12. "*For Emma read Betty.*" Ollier did not print "Peter Bell," and Shelley's injunction, being unknown to subsequent editors, was disregarded until Mr. Rossetti made the alteration in 1870. Shelley's delicacy is the more commendable, as Emma Hutchinson was only Wordsworth's sister-in-law.

P. 150, *l.* 16. "*Caloethes scribendi.*" "Peacock printed *cacoethes* for *caloethes*, apparently not perceiving Shelley's joke."—*Forman.* The allusion throughout is to Peacock's "Four Ages of Poetry," which called forth Shelley's "Defence."

P. 156, *l.* 16. "*A Greek prince.*" Prince Mavrocordato, to whom "Hellas" is dedicated.—"*The only Italian.*" Emilia Viviani.

P. 164, *l.* 1. "*One of the unpublished cantos of 'Don Juan.'*" The fifth; see the next letter.

P. 166, *l.* 16. "*Tita the Venetian.*" There is an interesting account of Tita Falcieri in Laurie's "Sketches of some distinguished Anglo-Indians," from which it appears that, after the death of Byron, with whom he continued to the last, he was successively in the service of Hobhouse, Mr. Isaac Disraeli, and Lord Beaconsfield, who obtained for him the situation of messenger at the India House. He died in 1874. He is said to have had many anecdotes of Shelley, but to have been reticent about Byron. Perhaps his last master's "Venetia" owes something to him.

P. 166, at bottom. "το δυσσεβες," etc. These lines are from the "Agamemnon" of Aeschylus, v. 728–30. They are expanded in the well-known quatrain in "Hellas":

"Revenge and wrong bring forth their kind,
The foul cubs like their parents are;
Their den is in the guilty mind,
And Conscience feeds them with despair."

P. 169, *l.* 16. "*A pamphlet signed John Bull.*" "This production much excited Lord Byron's curiosity. In one of his letters to Mr. Murray he asks, 'Who the devil can have done this diabolically well-written letter?' and subsequently he is found resting his suspicion on one of his own most intimate personal friends."—"Works of Lord Byron," 1833, vol. xv. p. 32.

P. 171, *l.* 1. "*Allegra.*" The daughter of Lord Byron and Miss Clairmont.

P. 177, l. 4. "*She has a specific purpose in the sum which she instructed me to require.*" To discharge a liability of Godwin's.——At bottom: "*Castruccio, Prince of Lucca.*" It was eventually published under the title of "Valperga."

P. 185, l. 3. "*A servant girl and her sweetheart.*" An allusion to Hazlitt's "Liber Amoris."——Line 6: "*A dramatic poem called 'Hellas.'*" "The title was suggested by Williams, who transcribed the poem for the press." *Forman.*

P. 190, l. 19. "*Our windows are full of plants, which turn the sunny winter into spring.*" These unquestionably inspired the "Magic Plant," and the "Zucca," written about this time.

P. 191, l. 5. "*Since you give me no encouragement about India.*" "He had expressed a desire to be employed politically at the court of a native prince, and I had told him that such employment was restricted to the regular service of the East India Company."—*Peacock.*

P. 192, l. 15. "*Ask Coleridge,*" etc. Coleridge told Mrs. Gisborne that he feared a faithful translation of "Faust" would not be tolerated, and that he would not mutilate it.

P. 197, l. 6. "*A satire upon satire.*" This fragment, of much personal but little poetical interest, was printed for the first time in Professor Dowden's edition of Southey's correspondence with Caroline Bowles, and has not yet been included among Shelley's works.

P. 198, at bottom. "*I want it for a present.*" No doubt to Mrs. Williams; and it may be concluded with equal certainty that the commission was not executed, and that the intended harp had to be represented by the guitar, bought, according to Trelawny's recollection, at Leghorn, and immortalised in the matchless verses beginning —

"Ariel to Miranda—Take
This slave of music, for the sake
Of him who is the slave of thee."

This explains the hitherto obscure allusion in letter L. —"I have contrived to get my musical coals at Newcastle itself."

P. 208, at bottom. *"Some adventurers are engaged upon a steam-boat at Leghorn to make the trajet we projected."* Shelley never renounced the idea. Williams notes in his diary, Jan. 6, 1822 :—" After a conversation with S. have serious thoughts of taking in hand a steam-yacht to work between Leghorn and Genoa."

P. 209, l. 13. *Mrs. Mason.* Lady Mountcashel, Mary Wollstonecraft's pupil, who lived at Pisa under this name.

P. 214, l. 21. "*He will be half mad to hear of these memoirs.*" A worthless anonymous compilation by a person named Watkins, entitled, " Memoirs of the Life and Writings of the Right Honourable Lord Byron, with Anecdotes of some of his Contemporaries." London, 1822. Shelley is therein designated as "Byron's chief disciple."

P. 215, l. 21. "*If the past and the future could be obliterated.*"

"The past and future were forgot
As they had been, and would be, not."
Lines in the Bay of Lerici,
written nearly at this time.

P. 223. Some extracts from this letter, derived from a transcript by Mr. Gisborne, were published by the editor of this volume in the *Fortnightly Review* for June, 1878; and the whole of it was printed from the original by Mr. Forman in *Macmillan's Magazine* for June, 1880, and subsequently republished in the fourth volume of his edition of Shelley's prose works. He has adhered to the MS. with scrupulous fidelity, except for some trifling changes in orthography and punctuation. A few more orthographical corrections have been made in the present recension, and the punctuation has been recast throughout.

P. 227, *l.* 21. "*How long do you mean to be content?*" See the letter to Gisborne of June 18, at p. 215 of this selection, which makes it evident that the vision was inspired by Shelley's study of "Faust," and not, as previously stated, by a scene in Calderon.

P. 229, at bottom. "*San Terenzo.*" Mrs. Shelley always writes the name of the hamlet near which Shelley resided *Sant' Arenzo;* Mr. Forman shows that according to the most recent maps and the Italian post office it should be *San Terenzio* or *San Terenzo*, and Mr. Alfred Austin, in a letter to the *Athenæum* of April 29 of the present year, says that this form is a corruption of *Sant' Erenzo*. No such saint as *Arenzo* or *Erenzo* is to be found in the calendar, but *Terenzio* or *Terenzo* does exist there, although it may be questioned whether he ever existed anywhere else. He is the patron saint of Pesaro, his festival is on September 24, and there is a special office in his honour, printed in 1592 and several times subsequently. The legendary character of his acts, according to which he suffered martyrdom under a petty Pannonian king named Dagnus, during the persecution of the Emperor Decius, has been demonstrated by Annibale Giordani in his treatise *Di San Terenzio Martire*, Pesaro, 1776. They appear to be a fabrication of the thirteenth or fourteenth century. The improbability of so very obscure a saint, patron of a town on the Adriatic, having given name to a village on the Gulf of Spezzia, may perhaps warrant the conjecture that the name was originally Santo Lorenzo, contracted into Santo Renzo, and corrupted into Sant' Arenzo. It has been thought best on the whole to adopt the orthography in the text, as being, according to Mr. Austin, that at present recognised by the Italian post office.

P. 235. l. 16. "*The haze of the storm hid them from me, and I saw them no more.*" "It was almost dark, although only half-past six o'clock. The sea was of the colour, and looked as solid and smooth as a sheet of lead, and covered with an oily scum. Gusts of wind swept over without ruffling it, and big drops of rain fell on its surface, rebounding, as if they could not penetrate it."— *Trelawny*, "Recollections," p. 117. There is a wonderfully prophetic anticipation of the catastrophe in Mrs. Shelley's "Valperga," which was indeed not published until 1823, but which, as appears by letters from Shelley to Horace Smith and Mrs. Godwin, was completed and in Godwin's hands before May, 1822. The fate of the heroine,

Euthanasia (the very name seems prophetic) is thus described:

"Euthanasia stepped into the boat; its commander sat beside her; and the men took their oars; she waved her hand to her guide saying, 'Farewell, may God bless you!' she added in a low tone, half to herself—'They speak Italian also in Sicily.'

"These were the last words she ever spoke to any one who returned to tell the tale. The countryman stood upon the beach; he saw the boat moor beside the vessel; he saw its crew ascend the dark sides. The boat was drawn up; the sails were set; and they bore out to sea, receding slowly with many tacks, for the wind was contrary; the vessel faded on the sight; and he turned about and speeded to Lucca.

"The wind changed to a more northerly direction during the night; and the land-breeze of the morning filled their sails, so that, although slowly, they dropt down southward. About noon they met a Pisan vessel, who bade them beware of a Genoese squadron, which was cruising off Corsica: so they bore in nearer to the shore. At sunset that day a fierce scirocco rose, accompanied by thunder and lightning, such as is seldom seen during the winter season. Presently they saw huge dark columns, descending from heaven, and meeting the sea, which boiled beneath; they were borne on by the storm, and scattered by the wind. The rain came down in sheets; and the hail clattered, as it fell to its grave in the ocean; the ocean was lashed into such waves that, many miles inland, during the pauses of the wind, the hoarse and constant murmurs of the far-off sea made the well-housed landsman mutter one more prayer for those exposed to its fury.

"Such was the storm, as it was seen from shore. Nothing more was ever known of the Sicilian vessel which bore Euthanasia. It never reached its destined port, nor were any of those on board ever after seen. The sentinels who watched near Vado, a town on the sea beach of the Maremma, found on the following day that the waves had washed on shore some of the wrecks of a vessel; they picked up a few planks and a broken mast, round which, tangled with some of its cordage, was a white silk handkerchief, such a one as had bound the tresses of Euthanasia the night that she had embarked, and in its knot were a few golden hairs."

www.ingramcontent.com/pod-product-compliance
Lightning Source LLC
Chambersburg PA
CBHW031959230426
43672CB00010B/2204